The Pocket Guide to Key Terms for Beauty Therapy

Lorraine Nordmann
Marian Newman

Australia • Brazil • Japan • Korea • Mexico • Singapore • Spain • United Kingdom • United States

The Pocket Guide to Key Terms for Beauty Therapy Lorraine Nordmann and Marian Newman Publishing Director: Linden Harris Publisher: Lucy Mills Development Editor: Helen Green Production Editor: Lucy Arthy Editorial Assistant: Claire Napoli Production Controller: Eyvett Davis Marketing Executive: Lauren Mottram Typesetter: MPS Limited, a Macmillan company Cover design: Adam Renvoize	© 2012, Cengage Learning EMEA ALL RIGHTS RESERVED. No part of this work covered by the copyright herein may be reproduced, transmitted, stored or used in any form or by any means graphic, electronic, or mechanical, including but not limited to photocopying, recording, scanning, digitizing, taping, Web distribution, information networks, or information storage and retrieval systems, except as permitted under Section 107 or 108 of the 1976 United States Copyright Act, or applicable copyright law of another jurisdiction, without the prior written permission of the publisher. While the publisher has taken all reasonable care in the preparation of this book, the publisher makes no representation, express or implied, with regard to the accuracy of the information contained in this book and cannot accept any legal responsibility or liability for any errors or omissions from the book or the consequences thereof. Products and services that are referred to in this book may be either trademarks and/or registered trademarks of their respective owners. The publishers and author/s make no claim to these trademarks. The publisher does not endorse, and accepts no responsibility or liability for, incorrect or defamatory content contained in hyperlinked material.

> For product information and technology assistance,
> contact **emea.info@cengage.com**.
> For permission to use material from this text or product,
> and for permission queries, email **emea.permissions@cengage.com**.

This work is adapted from *Beauty Basics 3e, Beauty Therapy: The Foundations 5e, Professional Beauty Therapy 4e* and *The Complete Nail Technician 3e*, published by Cengage Learning, Inc. © 2011.

British Library Cataloguing-in-Publication Data
A catalogue record for this book is available from the British Library.

ISBN: 978-1-4080-6040-7

Cengage Learning EMEA
Cheriton House, North Way, Andover, Hampshire, SP10 5BE United Kingdom

Cengage Learning products are represented in Canada by Nelson Education Ltd.

For your lifelong learning solutions, visit **www.cengage.co.uk**

Purchase your next print book, e-book or e-chapter at **www.cengagebrain.com**

Printed in China by RR Donnelley
2 3 4 5 6 7 8 9 10 – 15 14 13

Introduction to the Pocket Guide to Key Terms for Beauty Therapy

The vocabulary associated with beauty therapy can be complicated and might seem daunting at first. This *Pocket Guide* aims to provide you with quick and simple definitions to all the key terms you will encounter throughout your studies.

The Pocket Guide to Key Terms for Beauty Therapy is designed to sit alongside our leading series of Beauty Therapy textbooks by Lorraine Nordmann and our key Nail textbook by Marian Newman as a handy reference guide and easy-to-use revision tool.

Beauty Basics: The Official Guide to Beauty Therapy Level 1, 3rd edition
Lorraine Nordmann
9781408019351
£16.99 (September 2010)

Beauty Therapy: The Foundations: The Official Guide to Beauty Therapy Level 2, 5th edition
Lorraine Nordmann
9781408019368
£25.99 (March 2010)

Professional Beauty Therapy: The Official Guide to Beauty Therapy Level 3, 4th edition
Lorraine Nordmann
9781408019283
£33.99 (June 2010)

Complete Nail Technician, 3rd edition
Marian Newman
9781408032442
£31.99 (April 2011)

Beauty Therapy: The Foundations: The Official Guide to VRQ Level 2, 5th edition
Lorraine Nordmann
9781408054963
£25.99 (February 2012)

These market leading textbooks have been fully revised and updated to reflect the latest National Occupational Standards at Level 1, 2 and 3 and are the only guides to beauty therapy fully endorsed by Habia.

Buy your copies online now at **www.cengagebrain.com**.

A

Abduction To move the body part (limb) away from the centre of the body.

Abrasive Material used to shape, polish and remove the surface of natural and artificial nails.

ABS Acrylonitrile-butadiene-styrene; a plastic; a polymer or resin from which most plastic nail tips are made.

Absorption The ability to absorb (soak up or take-in); one of the main 'routes of entry' into the body is absorption through the skin.

Accident book Health and safety legislation requires that a written record is kept of any reportable injury, disease or dangerous occurrence in the workplace. This can be recorded in an accident book. Incidents in the accident book should be reviewed to see where improvements to safe working practices could be made.

Accident form A detailed report form to be completed following any accident in the workplace.

Acetone A solvent commonly used as a tip remover and nail polish remover.

Acid mantle The combination of sweat and sebum on the skin's surface which creates an acid film. The acid mantle is protective and discourages the growth of bacteria and fungi. The pH scale is used to measure the acidity or alkalinity of a substance using a numbered scale. The skin's pH is acidic at 5.5–5.6.

Acids Substances that have pH values of less than 7.0; the opposite of alkaline.

Acrylates Monomers used in UV light cured gel products.

Acrylic powder Used in the application of artificial nails. It is a finely ground polymer, (made from many units of monomers) which is mixed with liquid monomer to form a strong acrylic.

Acrylics Nail enhancement systems use two components, liquid monomer and powder polymer, to create a type of plastic known as acrylic.

Activator One of the components in the 'fibre nail enhancement system'. This is a liquid that speeds up or activates the polymerisation of a cyanoacrylate resin.

Additional products and services Products and services offered by your workplace which a client may receive or purchase to enhance their service benefits.

Adduction To move the body part (limb) towards the centre of the body.

Adhesion A force that makes two surfaces stick together.

Adhesives Chemicals which create a specialized glue that enables two surfaces to stick together.

Adipose tissue A body tissue layer that stores fat.

Affusion shower A relaxation shower of warm droplets of water which may use aromatic products to create the experience of aromatic rain. It is received whilst lying on a treatment bed and manual massage may be incorporated with its application to improve blood and lymphatic circulation.

Aftercare advice Recommendations given to the client following a service to maintain the finished result or effect and enable the benefits to be continued at home.

After-wax lotion A product applied to the skin following hair removal to reduce redness and promote skin healing.

Age groups The classification of ages into different groups to help identify skin characteristics at different stages of life. e.g. 16–30, 31–50 and over 50 years.

Age related ridges Longitudinal lines on some or all nails.

AHA Alpha hydroxy acid. Relatively mild fruit acid used as an ingredient in some skincare products. It can assist with skin exfoliation and encourage healthy cell renewal.

Albinism A skin condition where the skin cells do not produce the pigment melanin.

Alkaline Substances that have pH values between 8-14; the opposite of acid.

Allergen A substance or material that the skin is sensitive to and causes an allergic reaction.

Allergic reaction The reaction of the body to a substance or material that could be harmful or that the body has developed a sensitivity to (e.g. nickel in metal). This reaction may be topical (restricted to an area) or systemic (affecting the whole body). Symptoms include erythema, swelling and itching.

Alternating current (ac) An interrupted electrical current which periodically reverses the direction of flow of electrons.

Amino acids Small molecules that the body uses as building blocks for proteins.

Anaemia A blood disorder affecting the blood's ability to transport oxygen, characterized by a deficiency in the nutrient iron. Symptoms can include tiredness and depression.

Anagen The stage of hair growth during which the hair is actively growing.

Anion A negatively charged ion. An atom that has gained more electrons than protons.

Anode A positive electrode or pole of a constant electrical current.

Anterior Situated before or at the front.

Anti-oxidant A molecule found in some foods that maintains the health of the skin by fighting the damaging effects of free radicals (unstable molecules which can cause skin cells to degenerate). Anti-oxidant ingredients are increasingly being included in skincare preparations to neutralize free radicals or repel them from the skin.

Antiseptic A chemical agent that prevents the multiplication of micro-organisms. It has a limited action and does not kill all micro-organisms.

Aorta The large artery in the body leading blood away from the heart.

Apocrine gland A sweat gland found in the armpit, nipple and groin area. It is larger than the eccrine sweat gland and is attached to the hair follicle. These sweat glands are controlled by hormones and become active at puberty.

Appointment

Appointment An arrangement made for a client to receive a service on a particular date and time.

Appraisal A process whereby a supervisor, referred to as an appraiser, identifies and discusses with an individual, their performance and achievements in their job role against previously set targets.

Aromatherapy The use of essential oils combined with massage to bring about a feeling of well-being.

Arrector pili muscle A small muscle attached to the hair follicle and base of the epidermis. When the muscle contracts (shortens) it causes the hair to stand upright in the hair follicle creating 'goose bumps'.

Art director The person who is in overall charge of the visual appearance and how it communicates to the target audience. They come up with the visual concepts for the design brief and communicate with everyone else involved in the process to ensure the 'vision' is realized.

Arteries Blood vessels that carry the blood from the heart to other parts of the body.

Arthritis A medical condition characterized by the inflammation of the body's joints.

Artificial lashes Threads of nylon fibre which are attached to the natural hair. These are referred to as strip lashes, individual artificial lashes and single lash extensions.

Artiste When working as a photographic and fashion make-up artist, these are the people on whom you are working such as musicians, dancers and actors.

Aseptic The process of implementing disinfecting and sterilization procedures to prevent contamination of tools and equipment which could lead to cross-infection.

Assessment Techniques used to assess the needs of the client to ascertain the service objectives, including questioning and natural observation.

Assessor A person qualified to assess the performance of a candidate.

Assistance The act of providing help and support.

Atom The smallest unit of matter that is recognisable as a chemical.

Atrium, right and left The two upper chambers of the heart that receive blood from the lungs and venous system of the body.

Atrophic scar tissue Scar tissue where the skin replaced at the site of the injury is diminished, and the skin at the scar area appears lower.

Audio sonic A hand-held electrical massage service applied to the face or body. The equipment produces sound waves, which vibrate through the skin's cells and tissues. The service is used for its physiological benefits on the skin and muscle tissues.

Autoclave An effective method of sterilization, suitable for small metal objects and beauty therapy tools. Water is boiled under increased pressure and reaches temperatures of 121–134°C.

Autonomic nerves Nerves that are not consciously controlled.

Autonomic nervous system (ANS) The part of the nervous system that is not under conscious control. The ANS controls the involuntarily functions of the body.

Avante-garde Meaning 'ahead of its time'. This is often referred to in fashion work in the hairdressing and beauty sector. It is also a popular category in hairdressing competition work.

Ayurveda (art of life) A sacred Hindu text written around 1800BC. In Ayurveda, life consists of body, mind and spirit – each person is different. By restoring balance and harmony of the body, mind and spirit, the health of the individual improves.

B

Back bubbling The bubbling of liquid and air into the cup of the airbrush during the mixing and cleaning processes. Colours are dropped into the cup and mixed using a technique called back bubbling. To do this you need to place a tissue over the tip of the airbrush and push down the trigger to release air. As it cannot flow out the end of the airbrush it will bubble back into the cup thus blending the shades together.

Bacteria Minute, single-celled organisms of various shapes. Large numbers live on the skin's surface and are non-pathogenic (not harmful); others, however, are pathogenic (harmful) and can cause disease.

Bacterial nail infection ('greenies') Bacteria forming between an artificial nail overlay and the nail plate. The bacteria causes a green stain on the nail plate.

Base coat A nail polish product applied to protect the natural nail and prevent staining from coloured nail polish.

Base note A measure of the evaporation rate of essential oils. Base notes have the slowest evaporation rate of all essential oils and are absorbed slowly into the skin.

Beaded ridges Longitudinal lines with little bumps found on the nail plate and usually associated with circulatory problems.

Beau's lines Horizontal lines on the nail plate.

Bed epithelium The epidermis that makes up the nail bed.

Behaviour This refers to how we conduct ourselves in the workplace. It is important to be be polite and friendly at all times, work cooperatively with others and conform with all workplace policies and procedures.

Benefit The gain to be made from using a product or service.

Benzoyl peroxide A heat-sensitive catalyst often found in powder polymers.

Bevelling A nail filing technique used at the free edge of the nail to ensure that it is smooth.

Bikini line (general waxing) Pubic hair is removed from the area that is visible at the top of the thighs and just under the navel when the client wears bikini briefs.

Blend epilation The use of both high frequency (alternating) current and galvanic (direct) current to combine heat and chemical effects for hair removal. Both currents retain their individual effects on the hair when applied.

Blending A nail art technique where coloured nail art paint is applied to the nail and using a nail art brush the colour(s) are blended to achieve different effects which will depend upon the type of nail art paints and colour applied.

Blepharitis Inflammation of the eyelid caused by an infection or an allergic reaction.

Blood A collection of specialized cells suspended in a liquid called plasma which circulate through blood vessels, supplying the needs of the body's cells to keep the body healthy. Blood transports essential nutrients and other important substances, such as oxygen and hormones, and removes waste products. Blood helps to maintain the body temperature at 36.8°C. Carrying blood nearer to the skin surface increases heat loss and cools the body.

Blood spots Small benign (non-cancerous) red spots often appearing on the chest or trunk caused by concentrations of blood underneath the skin's surface. This is medically termed haemangioma. Other names for these blood spots include Campbell de Morgan spots and cherry angioma because of their colour.

Blood vessels Part of the circulatory system that carries blood around the body. There are three main types of blood vessels: arteries; veins and capillaries which differ in their structure and role in blood transportation.

Blue nail A nail condition where the nail bed has a blue tinge rather than a healthy pink colour due to poor blood circulation in the area.

Blusher Make-up applied to add warmth to the face, emphasize the facial contours and draw attention to the cheekbones.

Body language Communication can be verbal or non-verbal. When we communicate non-verbally we use the body rather than speech. This is known as body language and includes how we use our eyes, face and body to transmit feelings and emotions.

Body wrapping A service where the body is wrapped in bandages, plastic sheets or thermal blankets to achieve different therapeutic effects including skin toning and weight loss.

Bone A specialized form of connective, structural tissue that supports, surrounds and connects different parts of the body. They have an important function of support, protection, movement, blood cell production and mineral storage. Bones are made of water, non-living (inorganic) material including calcium and phosphorus, and living (organic) material such as cells called osteoblasts.

Bones of the foot and lower leg A type of connective tissue that provides a surface for muscle attachment. In the foot these bones include the tarsals, metatarsal and phalanxes. In the lower leg the bones include the tibia and fibula.

Bones of the lower arm and hand A type of connective tissue that provides a surface for muscle attachment. In the lower arm, these bones include the radius and ulna. In the hand, these bones include the carpals, metacarpals and phalanges.

Bones of the chest A type of connective tissue that protects the inner organs and provides a surface for muscle attachment that allows movement. The bones in the chest include the sternum (breast bone) and the ribs.

Bones of the neck A type of connective tissue that supports the skull and forms the neck. The bones in the neck include the cervical vertebrae.

Brachial artery An artery of the arm.

Brittleness A characteristic which indicates how likely a substance is to break. This is often referred to following an assessment of hair or nails and is often a symptom of them being dry.

Bronzing products Make-up products applied to create a healthy, natural or subtle tanned look. They are formulated to create a matt or shimmer effect and are also maybe suitable as a highlighting and contouring product.

Bruised nail A nail condition where the nail appears blue/black in colour where bleeding has occurred on the nail bed following an injury.

Buff A technique applied to the skin and nails to achieve a smooth, even appearance.

Buffed The appearance of the nail following 'buffing' to create a sheen or achieve a smooth, even nail surface.

Buffer A manicure tool with a plastic handle and a pad with a replaceable cover. It is used on the nail to give a sheen and increase blood supply to the area. If used with a gritty cream buffing paste, a buffer can also help smooth out any nail surface irregularities.

Buffing mitt A specialized glove worn and used to remove excess tanning product and achieve an even tan result when performing a manual self-tanning service.

Buffing paste A coarse cream with a gritty texture which removes surface cells from the nail plate.

Bunion A foot condition. The large joint at the base of the big toe protrudes, forcing the big toe inwards towards the other toes.

Burn An injury to the skin caused by excessive heat. The skin appears red and may blister.

C

'C' curve The curve of the nail from side wall to side wall.

Calcaneus One of the tarsal bones in the foot. It is often referred to as the heel bone.

Caldarium A Roman-style steam room that uses natural herbal essences to create an aromatic atmosphere. These aromas have a therapeutic effect when inhaled.

Callus A foot condition. A callus is an area of thick, yellowish, hardened skin, usually found on prominent areas of the foot such as the heel. It is often caused by pressure or friction (rubbing).

Camouflage products Cosmetics used for remedial work to disguise blemishes or scars to the face or body.

Capillaries Small blood vessels that carry blood to all parts of the body.

Carbon dioxide A gaseous waste product of cell metabolism as a result of using oxygen in the body which is collected by the blood and expelled by the lungs when breathing out.

Cardiac muscle A type of muscle found only in the heart.

Cardiovascular The circulatory system in the body consisting of the heart and blood vessels which distributes blood to all parts of the body.

Care Standards Act (2000) You must comply with all your responsibilities under current health and safety legislation including the Care Standards Act. The Care Standards Act (2000) is the regulatory framework for social care to ensure high standards of care and protection of vulnerable people.

Carpals Bones found in the wrist.

Cartilage A strong fibrous connective tissue that helps support the body. Cartilage is found at the end and in between the joints.

Cartilaginous joints A type of joint which is slightly moveable and is made from cartilage that is softer than bone. An example is the nasal bone.

Catagen The stage of the hair growth cycle where the hair becomes detached from its source of nourishment (the dermal papilla) and stops growing.

Catalyst A chemical added to a substance to promote, speed or control the chemical reaction or polymerisation. A catalyst does not take part in the chemical reaction.

Cataphoresis This is usually applied after an electrical epilation service. A positive polarity galvanic current is used to produce an acid on the skin to sooth and reduce redness.

Cathode A negative electrode or pole of constant electrical current.

Cation A positive ion. An atom that has lost an electron and has more protons than electrons.

Cell Basic units of life which specialize in carrying out particular functions in the body. Groups of cells that share function, shape, size or structure are called tissues. The human body consists of trillions of cells.

Cellulite Fatty tissue that causes the overlying skin to appear dimpled.

Central nervous system (CNS) Part of the nervous system that includes the brain and spinal cord.

Certificate of registration Awarded when a premises have been successfully inspected to ensure that the local bye-laws are being followed in relation to cosmetic piercing.

Chakras Non-physical energy centres which cannot be seen and are located about an inch away from the physical body. It is an ancient Eastern belief that the body has seven major chakra centres, each with a specific function, that work together in balance with each other.

Charge card A form of payment where the complete amount of credit spent must be repaid by the cardholder each month to the card company.

Checklist A comprehensive list for verification purposes.

Chemical bond The bonds between the atoms and molecules of a chemical.

Chemical reaction A process where two or more chemicals combine to create a different substance.

Chemicals Matter. Everything except light and electricity is a chemical.

Cheque An alternative form of payment to using cash. A cheque must be accompanied by a cheque guarantee card.

Chilblains Poor blood supply where the toes become red, blue or purple in colour and the area may become painful and itchy. Chilblains are aggravated in cold weather.

Chiropodist Also known as a podiatrist. A practitioner qualified to give treatments to the feet that have a medical, rather than a cosmetic, focus.

Circulatory system The system that controls blood and lymph flow and transports material around the body. It supplies cells with oxygen and nutrients and carries away waste products.

Cleaning The removal of dirt, stains or anything else that could contaminate you, your client or the work area.

Cleanser A skincare preparation that removes dead skin cells, excess sweat and sebum, make-up and dirt from the skin's surface to maintain a healthy skin complexion. These are formulated to treat different skin types, skin characteristics and facial areas.

Client groups Used to recognize the diversity of the different clients you serve and to meet their different needs in line with the CRE (Commission for Racial Equality) ethnic group classification.

Clinical waste Waste materials that have come into contact with body fluids, e.g. waste from ear-piercing, which must be collected and disposed of by special arrangements. The disposal of clinical waste is controlled by the Environment Agency. The Environment Protection Act (1990) and the book *Waste Management: The Duty of Care, A Code of Practice* (ISBN 011752577X) provides further information on this subject.

Clippers A nail tool used to shorten the length of the toenail before filing.

CNS Central nervous system.

Code of conduct Workplace service standards with regard to appearance and behaviour while in the working environment.

Code of practice The expected standards and behaviour for the professional beauty therapist to follow, which will uphold the reputation of the industry, ensure best working practice and protect members of the public. Beauty therapy professional bodies produce codes of practice for their members. A business may have its own code of practice.

Cold wax A wax already applied to a strip and ready for use. The pre-coated strip is applied firmly to the skin and then removed quickly against hair growth, removing the hair from the area.

Collagen

Collagen A protein fibre providing strength to the skin and other types of connective tissue. They are produced by specialized cells called fibroblasts and are held in a gel called the ground substance.

Colour corrector A make-up product applied to target problem areas. It contains pigments which balance skin tone.

Colour theory The colour wheel consists of the three primary colours with the secondary colours in-between. The secondary colours are a mix of the two adjacent primary colours. In between the secondary colours on the colour wheel are the tertiary colours achieved by mixing the primary and secondary colours. Colour is reduced or removed by mixing colours that are directly opposite each other in the colour wheel.

Colouring characteristics Identified through consultation with the client and by examining the client's natural hair colouring (e.g. fair, red, dark and white) to determine the correct service plan e.g. selecting the appropriate tint colour for a permanent tinting treatment.

Comedone removal Facial techniques used to extract comedones (blackheads) from the skin. A small tool called a comedone extractor is used for this purpose.

Communication The exchange of information and the development of understanding between people.

Complaints procedure A formal, standardized approach adopted by the organization to handle any client grievances.

Compressor A piece of equipment used to compress air. The air pressure is then regulated by the attachment of a regulator. It is used in the application of make-up, nail art, airbrushing and self-tan.

Computer Electronic equipment that can be used to process and store data for the business.

Concealer A make-up product use to disguise small skin imperfections such as blemishes, uneven skin colour and dark circles under the eyes.

Conductor A substance that allows electricity and heat to move through it freely. Good conductors include metals and solutions which have conducting properties, such as acids and alkalis.

Confidential Information Data or information which is private. This may include a conversation that you have had with a client or colleague, client record card details or client and staff's personal information such as their addresses and telephone numbers.

Confidentiality Keeping information or data private. In order to gain trust between yourself and your client. It is important to keep client information confidential. This may also be a legal requirement stipulated by the Data Protection Act.

Conjunctivitis A bacterial infection. Inflammation of the mucous membrane that covers the eye and lines the eyelid. The skin of the inner conjunctiva of the eye becomes inflamed and the eye becomes very red, itchy and sore. Pus may exude from the eye area.

Connective tissue sheath Tissue that surrounds the hair follicle and

Consent form

sebaceous gland, providing both a sensory supply and a blood supply. The connective tissue sheath includes, and is a continuation of, the papilla.

Consent form Written permission obtained from a parent or guardian to perform a service on a client under 16 years of age.

Constriction Narrowing. This term is used when referring to the blood capillaries becoming narrower, which is also known as vaso-constriction. Constriction of the blood capillaries makes the skin look paler in colour as less blood is transported.

Consultation Assessment of a client's needs using techniques such as questioning and observation.

Consumer Protection (Distance Selling) Regulations (2000) These Regulations, as amended by the Consumer Protection (Distance Selling) (Amendment) Regulations (2005), are derived from a European Union directive and cover the supply of goods/services made between suppliers acting in a commercial capacity and consumers. These regulations affect purchases made by telephone, fax, internet, digital television and mail order.

Consumer Safety Act (1978) This Act aims to reduce consumers' risk from potentially dangerous products.

Contact area or well The area of a plastic tip that is adhered to the nail plate.

Contact dermatitis A skin disorder caused by intolerance of the skin to a particular substance, or a group of substances. On exposure to the substance the skin quickly becomes irritated and an allergic reaction occurs.

Contamination Unwanted or foreign substances on an implement, surface or in a product.

Continuous Professional Development (CPD) Activities undertaken to develop technical skills to ensure your experience is up-to-date and professional.

Contour cosmetics Products that change the shape of the face and the facial features. These cosmetics draw attention either towards or away from the shape of the face and specific facial features, helping create the optical illusion of balance and perfection.

Contra-action An adverse or unwanted reaction occurring during or after service application.

Contra-actions advice Recommended action to be taken to correct an adverse or unwanted reaction.

Contra-indication A present condition or restriction that means the service may not go ahead or may need to be adapted in some way.

Control of Noise at Work Regulations (2005) A safe working environment should be provided, therefore noise should be kept within safe levels. The employer has a duty to assess any noise risks in the workplace.

Control of risk The means by which identified risks are removed or reduced to acceptable levels.

Control of Substances Hazardous to Health (COSHH) Regulations (2002) (Including Biological Agents) Regulations Legislation that requires employers and the self-employed prevent or control the exposure of employees and clients to hazardous substances. This includes exposure to chemical cleaning/sterilizing agents and biological agents such as bacteria, fungi and viruses. Records of the COSHH assessment must be available for inspection.

Controlled Waste Regulations 1992 (as amended in 1993) Categorizes waste types. The Local Authority provides advice on how to dispose of waste types in compliance with the law.

Cooling systems Stone therapy uses stones that are chilled as well as heated. A cooling system refers to the method used to chill the stones such as stone cooler equipment or ice.

Corn Small areas of thickened skin on the foot which are often white in appearance and usually caused by pressure.

Corrosive Substances capable of causing rapid, and sometimes irreversible, damage to human tissue or other surfaces upon contact.

Cortex The thickest layer of the hair structure.

COSHH Control of Substances Hazardous to Health.

Cosmetic Products (Safety) Regulations (2004) Part of consumer legislation that requires that cosmetics and toiletries are safe in their formulation and are safe for use for their intended purpose as a cosmetic and comply with labelling requirements.

Cosmetic Products (Safety) Regulations (2008) Part of consumer protection legislation that requires that cosmetics and toiletries are safe in their formulation and are safe for use for their intended purpose as a cosmetic and comply with labelling requirements.

Credit card An alternative form of payment to using cash. These cards are held by those who have a credit account with a pre-arranged borrowing limit. Credit cards can only be used if your business has an arrangement to deal with the relevant credit card company.

Cross contamination The transfer of an infection directly from one person to another or indirectly from one person to a second person via an object.

Cross-infection The transfer of contagious micro-organisms by direct contact with another person or indirectly by contact with infected equipment.

Cure Polymerisation. When a liquid turns into a solid structure.

Curing The process of polymerisation.

Custom blended Mixing different product ingredients to achieve the client's service requirements e.g. mineral make-up face powder.

Customer care statement Defined customer service standards that are expected to be adhered to.

Cuticle (hair) The protective outer layer of the hair composed of a layer of thin, unpigmented, flat, scale-like cells. These cells contain hard keratin and overlap each other from the base to the tip of the hair.

Cuticle (nail) The overlapping epidermis around and extending onto the base of the nail, developing from the stratum corneum.

Cuticle cream or oil A cosmetic preparation used to condition the skin of the cuticle.

Cuticle knife A metal tool used on the nail to remove excess eponychium and perionychium (the extension of the skin of the cuticle found at the base of the nail).

Cuticle nippers A metal tool used to remove excess cuticle and neaten the skin around the cuticle area.

Cuticle remover A cosmetic preparation used to soften and loosen the skin cells and cuticle from the nail.

Cut-outs A technique used in unusual nail art that involves cutting away shapes into the plastic nail tip.

Cyanoacrylates The family of acrylates used in adhesives and resins.

Cyclical pattern of growth The hair growth cycle which can be divided into three phases: anagen, catagen and telogen.

Cyst A localized pocket of sebum that forms in the hair follicle or under the sebaceous glands in the skin. Cysts are semi-globular in shape, either raised or flat, and hard or soft. They are the same colour as the skin, or red if bacterial infection occurs.

Cytoplasm The gel-like contents of a living cell between the membrane and nucleus that holds the cell's structure.

D

Dangerous Substances and Preparations (Nickel) (Safety) Regulations (2005) Nickel has been found to cause allergies. It is important to check what metal is used for your supplier's ear-piercing jewellery and that it complies with these regulations.

Data Protection Act (1998) Legislation designed to protect client privacy and confidentiality.

Debit card A method of payment where the card authorizes immediate transfer of the cash amount from the client's account.

Decontamination The process of sterilising and disinfecting to reduce the risk of contamination and harm from pathogenic (disease forming) micro-organisms.

Deep cleanse Using a cleansing product – often a cream formulation – that will remain on the skin and allow massage movements to be applied to the skin to warm and reinforce the cleansing action.

Dehydrate A term used to refer to the removal of water. It is necessary to dehydrate the surface of the natural nail plate before a nail extension service. It can also be a facial skin characteristic, when the skin is lacking in water.

Demonstration An activity that allows you to show the client a product or service to enhance their awareness and understanding of it.

Deoxygenated blood Blood that is depleted of oxygen after travelling around the body before returning to the lungs.

Dermal papilla A small organ within the dermis that provide the hair follicle with blood necessary for hair growth.

Dermatitis An inflammatory skin disorder where the skin becomes red, itchy and swollen. There are two types of dermatitis. Primary dermatitis is caused when the skin is irritated by the action of a substance on the skin, and this leads to skin inflammation. Allergic contact dermatitis is where the skin is intolerant to a particular substance or groups of substances. Exposure to the substance will result in the skin quickly becoming irritated and an allergic reaction occurs.

Dermatosis papulosa nigra Multiple, benign, small, brown to black hyperpigmented papules, common among people with dark skin.

Dermis The inner portion of the skin, situated underneath the epidermis, which is composed of dense connective tissue containing other structures such as the lymphatic system, blood vessels and nerves. It is much thicker than the epidermis.

Desincrustation The ionization of a solution forming alkalis during galvanic therapy which softens dead skin and the fatty acids of sebum. It is used to achieve a cleansing action.

Desquamation The shedding of non-living cells.

Diabetes A disease that prevents sufferers breaking down consumed sugars and carbohydrates. Insulin, a hormone produced by the pancreas organ, is not produced in sufficient quantities to regulate the sugars and carbohydrates, resulting in excess sugar in the blood.

Diathermy Uses a high frequency alternating oscillating current, oscillating at millions of cycles per second. The current is introduced into the skin via a needle which produces heat as the water molecules in the cells are agitated by the high frequency energy.

Digestive system The system which breaks down food into nutrients that can be absorbed by the body into the bloodstream.

Digital arteries and veins Blood vessels found in the fingers.

Dihydroxyacetone (DHA) The active ingredient in self-tan products. DHA is a colourless sugar which reacts with amino acids in the skin to create a pigmented, tanned look.

Dilation Opening or widening.

Direct current (dc) An electrical current which uses the effects of polarity. The electrons flow constantly, uninterrupted, in one direction.

Disability Discrimination Act (1996) Legislation implemented to prevent disabled persons being discriminated against. Employers have a responsibility to remove physical barriers and to adjust working conditions to prevent discrimination on the basis of an employee having a disability.

Discrepancy A disagreement over amounts of money etc. This is referred to in instances where a client disagrees with what they are being asked to pay or the amount of change received.

Disease An unhealthy condition of the body.

Disinfectant The use of substances capable of killing some micro-organisms and inhibiting the growth of others. It is the second level of decontamination.

Disinfecting hands This refers to washing the hands with a liquid detergent with disinfectant properties to reduce the risk of contamination. A disinfecting hand gel is a popular product to apply following hand washing.

Disinfection A level of decontamination that kills some living organisms and inhibits the growth of others. It is suitable for hard surfaces and implements.

Disposable applicator A piece of equipment used to apply wax hygienically to the area of hair removal without contaminating the wax flowing back into the tube/container following application. The applicator head is thrown away after each service.

Distal An anatomical term meaning furthest away. It refers to the part of a structure that is furthest from the centre of the body.

Dorsal Relating or belonging to the back, e.g. the back of the hand.

Dry flotation A type of hydrotherapy that allows the client to experience a relaxing feeling of total weightlessness. The client is supported on a membrane covering a tank of water so that there is no contact with the water. The membrane supports the client's body weight without creating pressure points. Therapeutic skin care products may be applied to the skin, which is then wrapped to maintain heat and absorb the products.

E

Ear-piercing The perforation of the skin and underlying tissue of the earlobe to create a hole where jewellery can be inserted.

Eccrine glands One of two types of sweat glands found in the skin. The other type of sweat gland is the apocrine gland. Eccrine glands are tiny tubes which are straight in the epidermis, and coiled in the dermis. They are simple sweat-producing glands which are responsive to heat and are found all over the body, except in the armpit and groin, and help eliminate waste products and control body temperature.

Ectomorph A body figure type, usually with long limbs and a slender body.

Eczema A skin condition which appears as a reddening of the skin accompanied by itching and sometimes blisters. The blisters can leak tissue fluid which later hardens, forming scabs.

Eczema of the nail Inflammation of the skin, causing changes to the nail including ridges, pitting, nail separation and nail thickening.

Effleurage A stroking massage manipulation. It is used to begin the massage, as a link manipulation and to complete the massage sequence. It is applied in a rhythmic, continuous manner and induces relaxation.

Eggshell nail A nail condition where thin, fragile white nails curve under at the free edge.

Elastins A protein fibre found in the dermis of the skin that helps the skin maintain its elastic properties and return to shape. They are produced by specialized cells called fibroblasts, and are held in a gel called the ground substance.

Electric current The flow of electrons along an electric circuit between the electrical supply and the appliance.

Electricity at Work Regulations (1989) These health and safety regulations state that every piece of equipment in the workplace should be tested every 12 months by a qualified electrician. It covers the installation, maintenance and use of electrical equipment. It is the responsibility of the employer to keep records of the equipment tested and the date it was checked in order to keep it in a safe condition.

Electrolysis The total destruction of the follicle to prevent hair growth by using the chemical reactions created by a direct current. When electric current is passed through water containing ions (atoms carrying an electrical charge), the ions are made to move. Positive ions – cations – are attracted to the negative electrode, called the cathode. Negative ions – anions – are attracted to the positive electrode, called the anode. When the ions arrive at their respective electrodes, chemical reactions occur. Acids are formed at the anode and alkalis form at the cathode. This process is called electrolysis.

Electrolyte A solution containing electrically charged particles capable of conducting electricity.

Electro-muscle stimulation (EMS) An electrical service applied to both the face and body to specifically exercise muscles by using an electrical current to create a tightening, toning effect.

Electrotherapy The use of mechanical or electrical equipment to improve the condition and appearance of the face and/or body.

Elements The smallest part of a chemical that can recognisably exist. It consists of one type of atom, e.g. gold or copper.

Embedding A technique used in nail art that uses small items within the overlay.

Emery board A nail file used to shape the free edge of the nail.

Employers' Liability (Compulsory Insurance) Act (1969) This ensures the provision of financial compensation to an employee if they are injured as a result of an accident in the workplace. A certificate indicating that a policy of insurance has been purchased should be displayed.

Endocrine system A system that co-ordinates and regulates processes in the body by means of chemicals (hormones) released by endocrine glands into the bloodstream. Hormones control activities such as growth or the development of the secondary sexual characteristics.

Endomorph A body figure type, usually with short limbs and a plump, rounded body which is pear-shaped.

Enquiry A question presented by clients or business contacts to find out more information.

Environmental conditions The surroundings in which the service will be performed which should be the correct level at all times. This includes heating, lighting, ventilation and general comfort requirements for the workplace or service.

Epidermis The outer layer of the skin located directly above the dermis. The epidermis is composed of five layers with the surface layer forming the outer skin which has a protective function.

Epilation A form of hair removal. Electrical epilation uses an electrical current to permanently destroy the hair follicle tissue, preventing hair growth.

Eponychium The skin fold and seal that is found at the base of the nail plate.

Equal opportunity Non-discrimination on the basis of sex, race, disability, age, etc.

Equal Opportunity Policy The Equal Opportunity Commission (EOC) states it is best practice for the workplace to have a written Equal Opportunity Policy. This will include a statement of the employer's commitment to equal opportunities and the structure for implementing the policy.

Equipment or tools Apparatus used for a particular purpose within a service that enables the service to be completed.

Erythema Reddening of the skin caused by increased blood circulation to the area.

Essential oils The aromatic substances used in aromatherapy. They have an infinite range of aromas extracted from flowers, seeds, roots, fruits and bark. Different essential oils can produce different feelings and aromatic effects for a client.

Ethyl cyanoacrylate One of the acrylate-based family of adhesives, usually used as a nail adhesive.

Ethyl methacrylate (EMA) A monomer most commonly used in acrylic nail systems.

Evaluation A method of gaining feedback to measure the success or effectiveness of an activity or service.

Evaporation The conversion of a liquid into a vapour.

Exfoliant A cosmetic service used to remove dead skin cells from the skin's surface and accelerate the process of natural skin loss – called desquamation. This achieves a skin cleaning, rejuvenating action. It is applied to the face after facial cleansing and steaming or to the skin of the hands and feet, and the body prior to a self-tanning treatment. This process can be achieved by using a specialized cosmetic by using facial equipment where a brush is rotated over the skin's surface.

Exothermic A heat-producing chemical reaction.

Extensions Artificial structures applied to extend the length of a fingernail.

Extensor An anatomical term describing the action to extend or straighten.

External ear structure The outer part of the ear funnels sound waves inside the ear to enable hearing. It comprizes the pinna, lobe, cartilage and cartilaginous tissue.

Eye services

Eye services Services applied to the eye area to enhance the appearance of the eye.

Eye shadow Cosmetic make-up applied to the eye to complement the natural eye colour, to give definition to the eye area and create balance to the face.

Eyebrow colour Cosmetic applied to the eyebrow area to emphasize the eyebrows, alter their shape, and make sparse eyebrows look thicker by filling in any gaps with colour.

Eyebrow shaping Involves the removal of eyebrow hair to create a new shape (reshape) or to remove stray hairs to maintain the existing brow shape (maintenance). Small metal tools, called tweezers, are used to remove the eyebrow hairs.

Eyelash adhesive Specialized glue used to apply artificial strip eyelashes and individual eyelashes to the natural eyelash hair.

Eyelash and eyebrow tinting The permanent colouring of the eyelash or eyebrow hair to enhance their appearance by using a dye especially formulated for use around the delicate eye area.

Eyelash extensions Threads of artificial hair are attached to the natural eyelashes to make them appear thicker and longer.

Eyelash perming Involves using a chemical process to permanently curl the lashes which enhances the appearance of the eyes. The lashes immediately appear longer which suits most clients.

Eyeliner Make-up applied to define and emphasize the eyelid area directly above or below the eyelash hair.

F

Fabric mesh Usually a silk or fibreglass fabric used in a fabric nail extension 'system' to provide extra strength.

Face shape The size and shape of the facial bone structure. Face shapes include oval, round, square, heart, diamond, oblong and pear.

Facial A service applied to the skin of the face to improve the appearance, condition and functioning of the skin and its underlying structures.

Facial bones A type of connective tissue forming a hard structure that forms the face and forms an attachment point for muscles. These include the zygomatic, mandible, maxilla, nasal, vomer, turbinate, lacrimal and palatine.

Facial features The size of a person's nose, eyes, forehead, chin, neck, etc. When applying make-up products, make-up application can emphasize or minimize the appearance of facial features.

Facial products Skincare products used for a facial service which have specific benefits to care for and improve the function and appearance of the skin.

False eyelashes Threads of nylon fibre or real hair attached to the natural eyelash hair. There are two main types: individual or strip.

Fan-shaped nail A nail plate that is wider at the free edge than at the cuticle.

Faradic current An alternating current which is used in electrotherapy services to cause nerve and muscle stimulation.

Faradic service Also known as electro-muscle stimulation. This is an electrotherapy service applied to both the face and body. An electrical current is used to exercise muscles by stimulation, which creates a tightening and toning effect.

Faux tan An alternative word for the artificial suntanned effect achieved with self-tanning products.

Features The uniqueness or individuality of a product or service.

Femoral artery The main artery in the upper leg.

Femur A bone of the upper leg.

Fibres These are found in the dermis and give the skin its strength and elasticity. Yellow elastin gives the skin its elasticity and white collagen fibres gives skin its strength.

Fibreglass A plastic reinforced by fine fibres of glass. A fine mesh of fibreglass is used to strengthen a cyanoacrylate resin nail system.

Fibula A bone of the lower leg.

Fibroma A benign tumour of fibrous connective tissue.

Filaments A structure in striated muscle.

Finished sauna A timber construction where the air inside is heated to produce therapeutic effects. The heat induces sweating to cleanse the skin of impurities.

Fire Precautions Act (1971) Legislation that states that all staff must be familiar with, and trained in, fire and emergency evacuation procedures for their workplace.

Fitzpatrick Classification System Devised in 1975 at Harvard University, the Fitzpatrick skin classification scale can be used to categorize skin types, from a scale of 1 to 6, to measure the skin's ability to tolerate Ultra-Violet exposure. Type 1 being the least tolerant to UV exposure and type 6 being the most tolerant.

Flexibility The property of a substance that determines how much it will bend.

Flexor An anatomical term describing the action to flex of bend.

Flotation A spa service where the body is suspended in water (wet flotation) or supported on water (dry flotation) to induce relaxation.

Foam bath A shallow bath of water containing a foaming agent that surrounds the body, achieving a thermal effect. Increased perspiration caused by this effect aids the elimination of wastes and toxins.

Foiling A nail art technique that uses a foil to decorate the nails.

Follicles The hair follicle is where the hair is formed and grows. It is found in the dermis layer of the skin.

Folliculitis A bacterial infection where pustules develop in the skin tissue around the hair follicle.

Foot and nail services Specialized products and equipment designed to improve the condition and appearance of different nail and skin conditions.

Foot cream/oil A cosmetic mixture of waxes and oils applied to soften the skin of the feet and cuticles.

Foot rasp A pedicure tool used to remove excess dead skin from the foot.

Foot spa A foot bath incorporating massage and water aeration to create a bubbling effect that cleanses and relaxes the feet.

Foundation A make-up product applied to produce an even skin tone, to disguise minor skin blemishes and as a contour cosmetic.

Free edge The part of the nail plate that grows beyond and extends past the end of the finger.

French manicure A method of painting nails using a white colour on the free edge and a natural colour, i.e. pink, over the nail bed.

French white tips Plastic artificial nail tips that are opaque white and applied to provide the French manicure effect.

Friction A massage manipulation which causes the skin and superficial structures to move together over the deeper, underlying structures. The movements help to break down fibrous thickening and fat deposits, and aid the removal of any non-medical oedemas (areas of fluid retention).

Fumes A gas or vapour that smells strongly or is dangerous to inhale.

Fungus (fungi) Microscopic plants which are parasites. Fungus feeds on the skin and the waste products of the skin. They are found on the skin's surface or they can attack deeper tissues leading to medical problems.

Furrows Longitudinal ridges appearing on the nail plate.

G

Galvanic current A constant direct current which creates chemical effects. Hair removal can be achieved using direct current with galvanic epilation. Galvanic therapy introduces therapeutic substances into the skin using a direct current to achieve skin cleansing and specific effects upon the skin surface and underlying tissues.

Galvanic epilation Hair removal using direct current. The needle from the electrical epilation machine is inserted into the follicle and direct current flows out over the length of the needle. Sodium hydroxide (lye) is formed in the moisture of the hair follicle. This chemically decomposes the follicle tissue and remains in the follicle to continue to destroy the cells.

Galvanic therapy Therapeutic substances are introduced into the skin using a direct current to achieve specific effects upon the skin's surface and underlying tissues.

Gel A thickened liquid which can refer to a thick adhesive or a UV-cured material.

Gel stage Refers to the start of the polymerisation process of an 'acrylic' system when the liquid and powder react forming a 'gel-like' substance before hardening or curing.

Gender dysforiac When a person believes they belong to the wrong gender.

Gift voucher A pre-payment method for beauty therapy services or retail sales.

Glue An adhesive that is protein-based, usually animal-derived (e.g. bones, hides, etc.)

Gold needle Gold is used in electrical epilation needles for the treatment of sensitive skin as it is a good conductor of electricity allowing for the smooth application of the current.

Greater London Council (General Powers) Act (1981) This act covers the London boroughs and relates to cosmetic piercing. It states that no person can carry out cosmetic piercing unless they and their business are registered. It also states what records are required to be kept.

Grievance A cause for concern or complaint.

Grit Used to describe the abrasiveness of files and buffers. The higher the number, the finer the abrasive. A level of no less than 240 grit should be used on the natural nail.

Gyratory massage An electrical body massage service which produces friction on the skin's surface creating a heating, stimulating effect.

H

Habia Hairdressing and Beauty Industry Authority.

Habit tic A habitual action that damages the matrix of a nail. Usually seen on the thumb where the forefinger picks at the nail fold.

Hair A long slender structure that grows out of, and is part of, the skin. Each hair is made up of dead skin cells, which contain the protein called keratin.

Hair follicle A structure or appendage in the skin formed from epidermal tissue. Cells move up the hair follicle from the hair bulb, changing in structure, to form the hair.

Hair growth cycle The cyclical pattern of hair growth which can be divided into three phases: anagen, catagen and telogen.

Hairless skin Areas of skin which has no hair follicles. Hairless skin is found on the palms of the hands and the soles of the foot.

Hairy moles Moles exhibiting coarse, terminal hairs from their surface.

Hairy skin Areas of skin with hair follicles producing hair.

Hamman A steam bath with a hot, moist aromatic atmosphere to purify and detox. Traditionally a communal bath, the bath house has a dome shaped central chamber and further chambers of differing temperatures leading from it. The hottest room is heated from the floor.

Hand and nail treatments Specialized products and equipment designed to improve the condition and appearance of different nail and skin conditions.

Hand cream/oil/lotion A cosmetic mixture of waxes, water and oils applied to soften the skin of the hands and nail cuticles.

Hand technique Hair removal using thread held and looped between both hands. This technique is commonly used by practitioners on themselves. It is also known as 'cat's cradle', 'double looped' and 'self-technique'.

Hangnail A nail condition where small pieces of epidermal skin protrude between the nail plate and nail wall. Hangnails are usually caused by dry skin and cuticles.

Hardness A measure of how resistant a substance is to a force.

HASAWA Health and Safety at Work Act. Legislation laying down the minimum standards of health, safety and welfare requirements in the workplace.

Hazard Something with the potential to cause harm.

Hazardous Relates to substances that may be capable of causing physical or health-related injury.

Health and Safety (Display Screen Equipment) Regulations (1992) These regulations cover the use of visual display units (VDUs) and computer screens. They specify acceptable levels of radiation emissions from the screen and identify correct working posture, seating position, permitted working heights and rest periods.

Health and Safety (First Aid) Regulations (1981) Legislation that states that workplaces must have appropriate and adequate first-aid provision.

Health and Safety (Information for Employees) Regulations (1989) These regulations require the employer to make health and safety information available to all employees via notices, posters and leaflets published by the Health and Safety Executive (HSE).

Health and Safety at Work Act (1974) Legislation that lays down the minimum standards of health, safety and welfare requirements in all workplaces.

Health and safety policy Each employer of more than five employees must have a written health and safety policy issued to their staff outlining their health and safety responsibilities.

Heart Part of the cardiovascular (circulatory) system. The heart is a muscular pump that keeps the blood circulating around the body.

Heat rash A reaction to heat exposure where the sweat ducts become blocked and sweat escapes into the epidermis. Red pimples occur and the skin becomes itchy.

Heat services These include sauna, steam and the relaxation room. During a heat service there is an increase in body temperature of about 1–2°C.

High-frequency A high-frequency current is an electrical current which moves backwards and forwards at very high speed. The current is termed as an alternating or oscillating current. This rapid backwards and forwards movement creates high-frequency vibrations over the skin's surface. High frequency may be applied directly or indirectly to stimulate, disinfect and heal the skin.

Highlighter A make-up product that draws attention to and emphasizes facial features.

Hirsutism hair A hair's growth pattern which is considered to be abnormal for

Histamine

the person's sex. It often refers to a female who's hair growth follows a male hair growth pattern. In this instance the hair growth type is terminal (thick, coarse and pigmented) in appearance when it should be a vellus (fine, downy and soft).

Histamine A chemical released when the skin comes into contact with a substance to which it is allergic. This causes a histamine reaction. This reaction is a defence mechanism to protect the skin against harm from the unwanted substance that causes irritation. Cells, called mast cells, burst and release histamine into the tissues when the skin is irritated. This causes the blood capillaries to dilate, which increases blood flow to limit skin damage and begin repair.

Hoof stick A nail tool used to gently push back the softened cuticles.

Hooked (or claw) nail A nail plate that has an extreme upper arch and curves under at the free edge.

Hormones Chemical messengers secreted by glands in the body that are released into and transported in the blood. They control the activity of many organs in the body, including the cells and glands in the skin.

Hospitality Friendliness and care provided to clients at reception. This includes welcoming the client and being helpful, offering refreshments and magazines and ensuring the client is comfortable while waiting in the reception area.

Hot wax A system of wax depilation used to remove hair from the skin. Hot wax cools and sets on contact with the skin. Hot wax is a blend of waxes, such as beeswax and resins, which keeps it flexible. Soothing ingredients are often included to avoid skin irritation.

Humerus A bone of the upper arm.

Humidity Moisture content in the air.

Hydro bath An acrylic bath which provides underwater massage through high-powdered jets. A hose can be used to manually direct water to stimulate blood and lymphatic circulation in specific areas.

Hydro pool A pool of warm water where air is forced through small openings and jets of air pass through the water, creating bubbles. These bubbles massage the skin from all directions. Jets can be incorporated to massage different body parts, for example the lower back, and water fountains can be used to massage the neck with the power of the water flow.

Hydrogen peroxide (H_2O_2) A chemical oxidant that contains available oxygen atoms and encourages chemical reactions.

Hydrotherapy Spa services where water is used for its therapeutic effect.

Hygiene The recommended standard of cleanliness necessary in the salon workplace to prevent cross-infection and secondary infection.

Hygiene requirements Necessary workplace hygiene required to prevent cross-infection and secondary infection as a result of contamination. The standards expected are stated in health and safety legislation, industry codes of practice or written policies and procedures specified by the workplace.

Hyperidrosis Overactivity of the sweat glands of the feet, hands and axillae (underarms).

Hyperpigmentation Increased or darker skin pigmentation (colouring) in an area due to an over production of melanin.

Hypertrichosis Excessive hair growth for a person's sex, age and race. It is usually due to abnormal conditions in the body caused by disease or injury.

Hypertrophic scar tissue Scar tissue where the replacement skin found at the site of the injury is increased causing the skin at the scar area to appear raised.

Hyponychium The distal edge of the nail bed. A seal between the nail plate and nail bed.

Hypopigmentation Loss of pigmentation (colouring) in an area.

I

Incompatibility This refers to chemicals and products that cannot be used together as it will result in an adverse reaction.

Indian head massage A massage service, traditionally practised in India, that is applied to the upper body using the hands. The massage helps to relieve stress and tension and create a feeling of well-being. Oils may be applied to the scalp and hair to improve its condition.

Induction An introductory activity delivered when you start or progress into a new job role to provide you with general and essential information related to the work environment, welfare and your job roles and responsibilities.

Industry Code of Practice Written procedures specified by the workplace.

Infections The communication of disease from one body to another. An infection is the colonization of a host organism by parasite species. If the condition is present, do not treat the client.

Infestation A condition where animal parasites live off and invade a host e.g. scabies.

Infill A treatment that compensates for the natural nail growth after the application of artificial nails. This is usually required 2–3 weeks after application.

Inflammation Swelling, heat and pain. Inflammation is a process by which the body's white blood cells and chemicals protect us from infection and foreign substances such as bacteria and viruses.

Infra-red A pre-heating service using infra-red rays. An infra-red service is usually used before massage application.

Ingestion One of the main 'routes of entry' into the body which is via the mouth.

Ingrowing hair A painful condition where a build-up of skin occurs at the upper end of the hair follicle, causing the hair to grow under the surface of the skin.

Ingrowing toenails A nail condition where the side of the nail penetrates the nail wall which can cause redness, inflammation and pus.

Inhalation One of the main 'routes of entry' into the body which involves the movement of air from the external environment via the mouth and into the lungs.

Initiator A chemical additive that starts a chemical process.

Inner epithelial root sheath This grows from the bottom of the hair follicle at the papilla. Both the hair and inner root sheath grow upward together until level with the sebaceous gland when it ceases to grow.

Instructional techniques Educational methods to teach a person a skill or develop their knowledge and understanding in a new area. These include demonstrations, use of instructional diagrams, verbal explanations and use of written instructions.

Insulators Poor conductors of electricity. These are often used to prevent the flow of electrons and include rubber, plastic and wood.

Intercellular fluid A clear fluid that bathes all cells of the body and supports cell function.

Intimate waxing The application and removal of depilatory wax and all terminal hair (dependent upon the sex of the client) from the pubis, the buttocks, between the buttocks, scrotum and labia area of the body.

Iontophoresis The introduction of water-soluble preparations into the skin during galvanic therapy to assist rehydration and cellular metabolism in the area.

Iron A mineral necessary for efficient oxygen transportation by the blood.

Irritants Substances capable of causing inflammation of the skin, eyes, nose, throat or lungs.

Irritation A description of a mild inflammatory condition.

Isometric contraction A muscle that does not alter its length when under tension.

Isotonic contraction A muscle that shortens in length when under tension.

J

Job description Written details of a person's specific job role, duties and responsibilities.

K

Keloids Overgrowths of scar tissue caused by excessive deposits of collagen. The skin appears raised, shiny and ridged.

Keratin A protein produced by cells in the epidermis called keratinocytes. Keratin makes the skin tough and reduces the passage of substances into the body. Hair and nails are made of keratin.

Keratinized A description of a skin or nail cell that has lost its living cell contents. The cell cytoplasm is replaced with the protein keratin.

Koilonychia A nail disease where the nails become flat and spoon-shaped.

L

Lamellar dystrophy Peeling or splitting layers of the nail plate.

Langalier index or Palintest balanced water index The method used to regularly test and maintain the water quality in spa whirlpools and swimming pools.

Lanugo hair Hair found on an unborn foetus which is usually shed at the eighth month of pregnancy.

Laser hair removal A permanent hair removal technique. Laser energy is passed through the skin which stops hair follicle activity through a process called photothermolysis.

Lateral An anatomical term referring to the side.

Lateral and medial plantar artery and vein Blood vessels in the foot.

Lateral nail fold Skin on either side of the nail plate.

Legislation Laws affecting the beauty therapy workplace relating to products and services, the business premises and environmental conditions, working practices and those employed.

Leucoderma Patches of skin that do not have any pigmentation.

Leuconychia A nail condition where white spots or marks appear on the nail plate. These are usually caused by trauma to the nail plate, bed or matrix but may be medically related.

Lifting The separation of an artificial nail overlay from the natural nail plate.

Ligaments Fibrous connective tissue that hold bones together and support joints.

Limbic system A system relating to emotions and memory. It consists of a group of structures that encircle the brain stem.

Limits of your own authority Your level of responsibility as written in your own job description and workplace policies.

Lip balm A lip moisturiser which may contain pigment.

Lip gloss Make-up applied to the lips to provide a moist, shiny look.

Lip liner Make-up used to outline the lip and create a balanced shape to suit the face.

Lip stain A make-up product which adds intense colour to the lips.

Lipid A natural fat produced by the skin. This helps to form part of the intercellular cement that holds keratinized skin cells together.

Lipstick Make-up applied to the lips to add colour and keep the lips in good condition.

Liquid The most common definition is a physical state, e.g. solid, gas, liquid. In the context of nail products, a liquid refers to the monomer in a two-component acrylic system.

Local Government (Miscellaneous Provisions) Act (1982) Legislation that requires that salons offering any form of skin piercing be registered with the local health authority. This registration includes both the beauty therapists who will be carrying out the service and the salon premises where the service will be carried out.

Local Government Act (2003) (section 120 and schedule 6) An amendment to the Local Government (Miscellaneous Provisions) Act (1982) to enable each authority to regulate businesses providing cosmetic body piercing. Each local authority can introduce its own bye-laws to set the standards for cosmetic piercing.

London Local Authorities Act (1991 and 2007) This act states that no person shall carry out cosmetic piercing at an establishment without obtaining a licence from a participating London council. Conditions can be attached to the licence, such as hygiene practices, age restrictions, etc.

Longitudinal ridges A nail condition where grooves appear in the nail plate, running along its length from the cuticle area to the free edge.

Low odour chemicals Substances that have a lower evaporation rate or are not so easily detected by the human sense of smell. These chemicals are sometimes used in the context of acrylic monomers.

Lower arch The curve of the lower part of the free edge when viewed from the side.

Lunula The whitish area at the base of the nail plate where keratinization of the cells is incomplete. This is often referred to as the 'half moon'.

Lymph A clear, straw-coloured liquid circulating in the lymph vessels and lymphatic system of the body and filtered out of the blood plasma. Its main function is to fight infection and remove waste.

Lymph node or gland A structure in the lymphatic system that filters lymph.

Lymph vessel Referred to as lymphatics. They transport lymph that flows through the lymphatic system from the tissues to the blood.

Lymphatic drainage equipment Tools used to specifically improve lymphatic circulation by removing non-medical excess tissue fluid both locally and generally.

Lymphatic system Closely connected to the circulatory system. Its primary function is defensive; to remove bacteria and foreign materials in order to prevent infection. The lymphatic system consists of the fluid lymph, the lymph vessels and the lymph nodes (or glands).

Lymphocytes One of the white blood cells.

Lymphoedema A constriction in a lymph vessel causing localized excess lymph fluid.

M

Macrophage A type of white blood cell that destroys harmful micro-organisms.

Maintain To keep.

Make-up Cosmetics applied to the skin on the face to enhance and accentuate, or to minimize facial features. Make-up products create balance to facial features.

Make-up occasion The event the make-up is to be applied for, e.g. day, evening, wedding etc.

Make-up products Different cosmetics available to suit different skin types, colour and conditions, e.g. sensitive or mature. Make-up products include concealing and contour cosmetics, foundations, translucent powders, eye shadows, eyeliners, brow liners, mascaras, lipsticks, lip glosses, lip liners etc.

Make-up service The application of make-up cosmetics to enhance the skin and facial features which maybe carried out to suit a particular occasion.

Management of Health and Safety at Work Regulations (1999) This legislation requires the employer to make formal arrangements for maintaining a safe, secure working environment under the Health and Safety at Work Act. This includes staff training for competently monitoring risks in the workplace, known as a risk assessment.

Manicure A service to care for and improve the condition and appearance of the hands, nails and skin.

Mantle The area of skin that covers the matrix or proximal nail fold.

Manual Handling Operations Regulations (1992) health and safety Legislation which requires the employer to carry out a risk assessment of all activities undertaken which involve manual handling (lifting and moving objects) with the aim being to provide training and resources to prevent personal injury caused by poor working practice.

Manufacturers' instructions Guidance issued by manufacturers or suppliers of products or equipment concerning their safe and efficient use.

Marbelling A nail art technique that mixes two or more nail polish colours together.

Marma (pressure point) Incorporated into Indian head massage, this is a pressure point application, based upon the principles and practice of Marma. Pressure is applied to the nerve junctures which stimulates vital energy points on the head, face and ears to improve circulation, relieve tiredness and induce relaxation. Marma pressure points also balance the body.

Mascara Make-up that enhances the natural eyelashes making them appear longer, changed in colour and/or thicker.

Mask A cosmetic preparation applied to the skin which contains different ingredients to treat and improve its condition including deep cleansing, toning, nourishing, rejuvenating or refreshing. A mask may be applied to the hands, feet and face.

Massage Manipulation of the soft tissues of the body using the hands to produce heat and stimulate the muscular, circulatory and nervous systems.

Massage manipulations Movements which are selected and applied according to the desired effect which may be stimulating, relaxing or toning. Massage manipulations include effleurage, petrissage, percussion (also known as tapotement) frictions and vibrations.

Massage medium A product used to suit the skin type to which it is to be applied, e.g. oil, cream or talc. The massage medium lubricates the skin and facilitates the manipulation of the soft tissues to benefit the skin condition.

Matrix (hair) This is the lower part of the hair bulb which comprizes actively dividing cells from which the hair is formed.

Matrix (nail) The growing area of the nail which is found at the bottom of the nail and sometimes referred to as the nail root. It is formed by the division of cells in this area, called mitosis, and is part of the stratum germinativum layer of the epidermis.

Medial An anatomical term relating to the middle.

Medial plantar artery and vein Blood vessels in the foot.

Melanin A pigment in the skin and hair created by cells called melanocytes. Melanin contributes to the colour of the skin and hair and helps to protect the lower layers of skin from ultra-violet damage.

Melanocytes Cells that produce the skin pigment melanin, which contributes to skin and hair colour.

Mental preparation This is a relaxation technique requiring the therapist to relax and clear the mind of all other distractions to allow them to fully focus on the service being provided. Mental preparation is important before performing massage services.

Mesomorph A body figure type, usually a muscular build with well-developed shoulders and slim hips (an inverted triangle shape).

Messages Communication of information to another person in written, electronic or verbal form.

Metacarpal arteries and veins Blood vessels in the hand.

Metacarpals Bones in the hand.

Metatarsals Bones in the foot.

Methacrylic acid An acid commonly used as a primer in many nail systems.

Method of payment Different forms of payment that may be accepted to pay for a product or service including cash, cash equivalents, cheques and payment cards.

Methyl methacrylate (MMA) A monomer no longer used as a component of an acrylic system except as a 'co-polymer' with ethyl methacrylate (EMA).

Micro-current Based on a modified direct current and creates similar effects to galvanic current. It is a direct current interrupted at low frequencies of one to a few hundred times per second.

Micro-current therapy An electrical service used on the face and body which achieves an immediate skin toning and firming effect.

Micro-dermabrasion A mechanical exfoliating service for use on the body or face. Microcrystals are applied under pressure over the skin's surface and gently break down the skin's cells to achieve a skin rejuvenating effect.

Middle note A measure of the evaporation rate of certain essential oils. Middle notes have a moderate evaporation rate and are absorbed into the skin fairly quickly.

Milium extraction A skincare technique used to extract milia (whiteheads) from the skin. A small tool called a milia extractor is used for this purpose which superficially pierces the epidermis allowing effective removal of the milia.

Mineral make-up Created from finely ground minerals (a process called micronization). It is used in the formulation of different make-up products.

Minor A person classed as a child who requires by law to have a guardian or parent present. In Scotland a minor is classed as someone under the age of 16. In England, Wales and Northern Ireland a minor is someone under the age of 18.

Mist Fine liquid particles produced by spraying.

Mitosis The process of cell division and reproduction.

Moisturiser A skincare preparation usually a formulation of oil and water that helps hydrate the skin by adding moisture and preventing the skin losing moisture. It can also give protection with the inclusion of UV and pollutant filters. Different moisturiser formulations should be used depending on when it is to be worn (e.g. during the day or evening) and to suit the skin type, age, facial characteristics and facial area.

Molecule An arrangement of two or more atoms to create a specific chemical.

Monomer One unit or molecule. Individual chemical units can react to form a polymer.

Moodboard Used to express your overall ideas through a collation or collage of images which have inspired or instigated innovation and creativity. A moodboard may include objects such as photographs, fabric swatches and make-up colour samples or anything that has progressed your ideas.

Motor nerves Nerves situated in a muscle tissue that act on information from the brain causing a particular response on a muscle or gland, typically muscle movement.

Motor point A location on the muscles where the motor nerve enters the muscle and can be most easily stimulated.

Mould A term often, and incorrectly, used to describe nail infections, usually pseudomonas (a green infection between the nail plate and overlay).

Mouth technique Hair removal using a thread where one part of the thread is anchored in the mouth and the other part is looped in the hands. This is the most commonly used technique, originating from the Far East and is also known as the Asian or single looped method.

MSDS Material Safety Data Sheets. These are forms that provide various information relating to safety issues.

Mucocutaneous A variation of skin that secretes mucous (a thick, slimy liquid) for either protection or lubrication.

Mucous membrane The internal body lining that secretes mucous.

Multiple sclerosis A disease associated with the nervous system that affects the ability of nerve cells in the brain and spinal cord to communicate with each other. It affects the parts of the body controlled by the nerves e.g. vision.

Muscle Contractile tissue responsible for movement of the body which is made up of a bundle of elastic fibres bound together in a sheath called the fascia. Muscular tissue contracts (shortens) and creates movement.

Muscle tone The normal degree of tension in healthy muscle.

Muscles of facial expression Muscles which, when contracted, pull the facial skin in a particular way to convey the emotions of the individual. These include: the frontalis, corrugators, temporalis, orbicularis oculi, levator labii, orbicularis oris, buccinators, risorius, mentalis, zygomaticus, masseter, depressor labii.

Muscles of the foot and lower leg The muscles of the foot work together to help move the body. The foot is moved by muscles in the lower leg which pull on tendons that attach the muscle to the bone.

Muscles of the lower arm and hand The hands and fingers are moved by muscles and tendons. The muscles that bend the wrist in towards the forearm are flexors; the extensors straighten the wrist and hand.

Muscles of the upper body These move the arm and include pectoralis and deltoid.

Muscles that move the neck These include sternocleido mastoid, platysma, trapezius.

Myofibrils Fibres found in muscle.

N

Nails Hard, horny, epidermal cells that form a shield at the end of the fingers and toes to protect the living nail bed underneath.

Nail art Nail decoration using a variety of techniques, products and materials.

Nail art techniques These are application styles and include dotting, striping, marbelling, enamelling, foiling and blending.

Nail bed The area of skin that lies directly under the nail and is protected by the nail plate.

Nail enamel A term sometimes used to describe a product applied to the nail to add colour. It is also referred to as laquer or polish.

Nail enhancements Lengthening, strengthening or repairing the nail using a nail enhancement system such as UV gel, liquid and powder or wrap.

Nail finish The product applied to the natural nail after a nail service to enhance its appearance such as buffing nails or nail polish application.

Nail growth Cells divide in the matrix and the nails grow forward over the nail bed until they reach the end of the finger. The nail cells harden as they grow through a process called keratinization.

Nail lacquer See nail enamel.

Nail plate The nail plate is a tough hard covering on top of the nail bed. It is composed of keratinized skin cells.

Nail polish A clear or coloured nail product that adds colour and protects the nail. Cream polish has a matt finish and requires a top coat application. Pearlized polish produces a frosted, shimmery appearance and a top coat is not required. Nail polish is also referred to as nail varnish and enamel.

Nail polish drier An aerosol or oil preparation applied following nail polish application to increase the speed at which the polish hardens.

Nail polish remover A solvent used to remove old nail polish and grease from the nails prior to applying polish.

Nail polish solvent A product used to thin nail polish and restore its consistency.

Nail strengthener A nail polish product that strengthens the nail plate which has a tendency to split.

Nail structure Composed for protection, the nail is made up of the following parts: nail plate, nail bed, matrix, cuticle, lunula, hyponychium, eponychium, nail wall, free edge, lateral nail fold.

Nail unit The area at the end of the finger that includes all parts of the fingernail.

Nail wraps Most commonly a fibre system that is used to overlay the natural nail. Nail wraps can refer to any system.

National Occupational Standards (NOS) The level and detail of the various competencies required by specific industry sectors that make a person capable of carrying out specific work, laid down by the industry sector.

National Occupational Standards for Beauty Therapy Standards that set the relevant performance objectives, range statements and knowledge specifications to support performance in the beauty therapy industry. These can be obtained from the Hairdressing and Beauty Industry Authority (Habia) website: www.habia.org.uk.

Natural nail The fingernail that is formed in the matrix to make the nail plate.

Natural nail overlays Artificial nail products used to coat a natural nail plate.

Necessary action The action taken or service modification required to deal safely with a contra-action or contra-indication.

Neck technique Hair removal using a thread where one part of the thread is anchored around the neck and the other part is looped in the hands. It is a substitute for the mouth technique. This technique originates from the Middle East and is also known as the Arabian or single looped method.

Negative skin sensitivity test A chemical test on the skin where the result produces no skin reaction. In this case you may proceed with the service.

Nerve A collection of single neurones (nerve cells) surrounded by a protective sheath through which impulses are transmitted between the brain or spinal cord and another part of the body.

Nervous system This system co-ordinates the activities of the body by responding to stimuli received by the sense organs.

Neurones Nerve cells which make up nervous tissue.

No-light gel Used with a nail wrap overlay nail enhancement system and uses a cyanoacrylate-based resin with activator. When the activator is sprayed on the resin the gel hardens.

Non-verbal communication Communicating using body language, i.e. using your eyes, face and body to transmit your feelings.

Nutrients Substances in a person's diet that provide nourishment to the body.

Nutrition The nourishment derived from food required for the body's growth, energy, repair and production.

NVQ National Vocational Qualification. A qualification based on the National Occupational Standards and strongly promoted by the Department for Education and Employment (SVQ in Scotland).

O

Objective The aim or purpose of an activity that can be measured to see if it has been met or not.

Odour A smell which can indicate the presence of a chemical. It is not an indication of the degree of danger or quantity of the chemical.

Oedema An abnormal accumulation of extra fluid under the skin or in the body tissues which causes swelling.

Olfactory system Located high inside the nose, the olfactory system is responsible for our sense of smell. When we breathe in aromas, nerve endings in the olfactory system are stimulated and relay messages to the brain which then cause the body to respond.

Oligomers Chains of monomers that are considerably shorter than a polymer.

Onychocryptosis An ingrowing nail.

Onychodermal band A seal between the nail plate and the hyponychium.

Onycholysis A nail condition where the nail plate separates from the nail bed.

Onychomadesis Loosening of the nail plate at the proximal nail fold usually due to trauma.

Onychomycosis A fungal infection causing lifting, discoloration or rotting of the nail plate.

Onychophagy A nail condition where a person bites their nails excessively.

Onychorrhexis Brittleness and longitudinal splitting of the nail plate which is often associated with furrows.

Opportunity An appropriate time, chance or favourable situation.

Optical brightener An additive that makes colours look brighter and white look whiter.

Orange stick A disposable wooden tool used to apply products around the cuticle and free edge of the nail and to remove products from their containers. Orange sticks can only be used once and must be thrown away after use.

Organizational requirements Beauty therapy procedures or work rules provided by the workplace management.

Outer epithelial root sheath This root sheath forms the hair follicle wall. It does not grow with the hair but is stationery and a continuation of the growing layer of the epidermis.

Oval Either a face shape description or a description of a free edge nail that is rounded in shape.

Overlay A thin coating applied in the nail extension service to provide strength. It can also be placed on a natural nail.

Oxygenated blood Blood carried from the lungs which is rich in oxygen.

P

Painting techniques Nail art techniques using specialized paints, tools and brushes to create different effects. Examples include free hand, striping, dotting and marbling.

Palmar arches Blood vessels in the hand connecting the radial and ulnar arteries.

Papillae Projections near the surface of the dermis which contain nerve endings and blood capillaries. They supply the upper epidermis with nutrition.

Papilloma Fibrous hypertrophy skin growth projecting from the skin surface and commonly referred to as a skin tag.

Paraffin wax A mineral wax heated and applied to the skin, popularly the hands and feet, to provide a warming effect. This improves skin functioning, aids the absorption of service products and helps to ease the discomfort of arthritic and rheumatic conditions.

Parkinson's disease A degenerative disorder of the central nervous system resulting in muscular stiffness and tremors.

Paronychia A bacterial infection caused by damage or a foreign body. Swelling, redness and pus appears in the cuticle area and surrounding nail wall.

Patella A bone protecting the knee joint which is also known as the kneecap.

Pathogen A micro-organism capable of causing disease.

Pedicure A service to care for and improve the condition and appearance of the skin and nails of the feet.

Peripheral nervous system (PNS) The nervous system of the body excluding the brain and spinal cord. The PNS consists of 31 pairs of spinal nerves and 12 pairs of cranial nerves which pass nerve impulses between the central nervous system and the body.

Personal presentation Employees in the workplace should always reflect the desired image of the profession they work in. This requires a high standard of personal hygiene to avoid causing cross-infection and because you are working in close proximity with people. personal protective equipment should be worn which includes clean clothing suitable for the workplace. Employers will advise on personal presentation requirements.

Personal Protective Equipment (PPE) at Work Regulations (1992) Legislation which requires employers to identify, through a risk assessment, those activities which require special protective equipment to be worn or used. Instructions should be provided on how the personal protective equipment should be used or worn in order to be effective.

Petrissage A massage manipulation where intermittent pressure is applied to the skin tissues and underlying structures. Petrissage improves muscle tone by the compression and relaxation of the muscle fibres.

Peyer's patches Lymphatic nodes in the the small intestine of the lymphatic system.

pH scale A scale used to measure the level of acidity or alkalinity of a substance. This scale goes from 0–14. In the range of 0–6.9, the lower the pH value, the greater the acidity. 1 is the most acidic. In the range above 7, the greater the pH value, the greater the alkalinity. 14 is the most alkaline pH. A pH of 7 is neutral meaning it is neither acid or alkaline.

Phalanges Bones in the fingers and toes.

Photoinitiator A chemical that responds to specific types of light to start a chemical reaction.

Photosensitizers Something that causes the skin to become UV-sensitive such as certain medication.

Photothermolysis An effect created when using a laser for hair removal. The melanin pigment that provides hair colour absorbs the laser energy, which is converted to heat, and at a sufficient temperature destroys the part of the hair follicle where the cells divide to create the hair.

Physical characteristics The individual features of each client to be considered when planning a service, e.g. height, weight, posture, muscle tone, age, health and skin condition.

Pigment A colouring matter or substance. The pigment in skin and hair is called melanin. The amount of pigment varies for each person, resulting in different skin and hair colour.

Pilo-sebaceous unit The structure in the skin's epidermis and dermis consisting of the hair follicle and its associated sebaceous gland.

Pitting A description of a nail plate which has small dips on the surface. It is often a sign of a related skin condition such as psoriasis.

Placement A stone therapy technique where stones are placed in a specific position on or underneath the body.

Plantar arch Blood vessels in the sole of the foot.

Plasma The yellow liquid part of blood which contains the blood cells.

PNS Peripheral nervous system. The nerves that extend from the brain and spinal cord and relay messages between the central nervous system (CNS) and the rest of the body.

Podiatrist An alternative name for a chiropodist or foot specialist.

Pointilism A micro-pigmentation technique where tiny dots of colour are implanted into an area of the skin's surface.

Polish secures Accessories used in nail art that stick to the nail using nail varnish.

Polymerization A chemical reaction that creates polymer chains from monomers or oligomers.

Polymers Very long chains of chemically bonded monomers or units. It can refer to the acrylics used in artificial nails. It can also refer hair that is made up of chains of amino acids.

Popliteal artery An artery in the leg.

Positive skin sensitivity test An allergic reaction to the skin test. The skin appears red, swollen and feels itchy. In this case you may not proceed with the service.

Posterior An anatomical term relating to the back.

Posture The position of the body, which varies from person to person. Good posture is when the body is in alignment. Correct posture enables you to work longer without becoming tired. It prevents muscle fatigue (tiredness) and stiff joints.

Powder Make-up cosmetic applied to set foundation, disguise minor skin blemishes and make the skin appear smoother and oil-free.

Power jet massage The use of water to provide massage in spa therapy. The power jet massage is also referred to as 'douche a' jet and blitz. Whilst the client is standing, a body massage is provided using alternating warm and cold water directed at the body parts through a high pressure hose. Power jet massage stimulates the blood and lymphatic circulation and relieves tension.

Ppm Parts per million. This is a general ratio measurement and can be used to describe the number of molecules of vapour in one million molecules of air.

Practitioner The person carrying out the treatment or service, e.g. beauty therapist, nail technician, spa or massage therapist.

Pre-blended oils Aromatherapy oils used in massage to meet the client's physical characteristics and emotional preferences, e.g. relaxation, uplifting or sense of well-being.

Pre-heat services Heat can be beneficial when applied before other body services because it makes the body's tissues and systems more receptive.

Preparation To get ready.

Pressure points The application of pressure on specific points of the head, face or body during massage service using the fingertips or thumbs. This helps to release blocked energy channels flowing through the body, improving the body's circulation, function and repair.

Pre-tailor To shape a plastic tip before application to create a better fit and shape.

Pre-wax lotion An antibacterial skin cleanser used to clean the skin before wax application.

Prices Act (1974) This act states that the price of products has to be displayed in order to prevent the buyer being misguided.

Primer (make-up) A cosmetic which provides a base for make-up and acts as a barrier to prevent the absorption of the products into the skin.

Primer (nail) A substance used to improve the adhesion between the nail plate and artificial nail products.

Prioritize To make a list of tasks that need to be carried out and arranging them in order of importance and urgency to determine which tasks should be carried out first.

Promotion A way of communicating products or services to increase sales. It is an activity carried out to benefit the business and to meet specified objectives.

Pronation An anatomical term describing a type of body movement where the body part faces downwards e.g. pronation of the hand turns the palm downwards by movement of the flexed forearm.

Protein Chemical substances created by the body from long chains of amino acids.

Provision and Use of Work Equipment Regulations (PUWER) (1998) Regulations which lay down important health and safety controls on the provision and use of equipment to prevent risk. The regulations state the duties required by employers and for users.

Proximal An anatomical term meaning nearest to. It refers to the part of the structure that is nearest to the centre of the body.

Proximal nail fold The fold of the epidermis covering the matrix and extending onto the nail plate.

PSI Often referred to as a feature in the sale of spray-guns. This means pounds per square inch and refers to the pressure of the air generated by the compressor. This requires adjustment of the pressure to create the result required.

Psoriasis An inflammatory, non-contagious skin disorder where there is an increased production of cells in the upper part of the skin, appearing as patches of itchy, red, flaky skin on the body.

Psoriasis of the nail An inflammatory condition where there is an increased production of cells in the upper part of the skin. Pitting occurs on the surface of the nail plate.

Pterygium A nail condition where the cuticle becomes thick and overgrown. The cuticle adheres to the nail plate and is stretched forward by nail growth which can lead to splitting of the cuticle.

Public liability insurance Insurance which protects employers and employees against the consequences of death or injury to a third party while on the premises.

Pulmonary Relating to the lungs.

Pulsing A malfunction which may occur during airbrushing as a result of improper airflow. Pulsing is also referred to as an application technique where the trigger of the airbrush is intermittently pressed to create different textured results.

Punctual Arriving at the correct time.

R

Race Relations Act (1976) This Act makes it unlawful to discriminate on the grounds of colour, race, nationality, ethnic or national origin.

Radial artery and vein An artery and vein in the lower arm.

Radius A bone in the lower arm.

REACH 2007 A European Union Regulation concerning the Registration, Evaluation, Authorization and Restriction of Chemicals. It operates alongside COSHH and is designed to improve the information provided by chemical manufacturers through the provision of adequate safety data sheets.

Rebalance Part of the maintenance procedure for artificial nails. The 'rebalance' involves replacing the 'apex' to the correct place, filling in the re-growth area at the cuticle and replacing the smile line to the correct place.

Reception An area in the salon where clients are received and their enquiries dealt with, either in person or by telephone.

Receptionist A person responsible for maintaining the reception area, scheduling appointments, dealing with enquiries, taking messages and handling payments.

Receptors A type of nerve cell that receives a stimulus.

Record cards Confidential cards recording the personal details of each client registered at the salon. These cards also record services a client received and retail product purchases. The information may be stored electronically on the salon's computer.

Regulatory Reform (Fire Safety) Order (2005) This legislation requires that the employer or designated 'responsible person' must carry out a risk assessment for the premises in relation to fire evacuation practice and procedures.

Relaxation room A room of ambient temperature (close to the body's own temperature) and often referred to by the Latin name tepidarium.

Relevant person An individual responsible for supervising you during a given task or service, or the person whom you are required to report things to.

Repetitive strain injury (RSI) An injury incurred through the repetitive movement of a particular part of the body.

Reporting of Injuries, Diseases and Dangerous Occurrences Regulations (RIDDOR) (1995) RIDDOR requires the salon or business to notify the HSE incident contact centre (ICC) in any case of personal injury, disease or dangerous incident in the workplace.

Reproductive system These systems include the male and female sex glands. The male testes which produce sperm required for sexual reproduction and the female ovaries which produces the egg required for sexual reproduction.

Resale Prices Acts (1964 and 1976) These acts state that the manufacturer can supply a recommended price (MRRP), but the seller is not obliged to sell at the recommended price.

Resin A version of cyanoacrylate used in the fibre nail enhancement system.

Resin activator A product that speeds up the cure time of a cyanoacrylate resin.

Resources The different products, equipment and other items needed to complete an activity or service.

Respiratory system The system which brings air into close contact with the blood in the lungs and enables oxygen to enter the bloodstream and be transported to all cells in the body where it can be used to provide energy by cell respiration.

Responsible persons A term used in the health and safety unit to mean the person or persons at work to whom you should report any issues, problems or hazards. This could be a supervisor, line manager or your employer.

Restriction Something that limits you. Certain contra-indications do not prevent a service but they restrict how the service is carried out.

Retail The selling of goods, e.g. products that clients use at home.

RIDDOR Reporting of Injuries, Diseases and Dangerous Occurrences Regulations.

Ridge-filler A nail product used on ridged nails that improves the nail's appearance and provides a more even surface.

Risk The likelihood of a hazard occurring.

Risk assessment A requisite of COSHH that requires employers organize for the assessment of potential hazards in the workplace.

Roller wax A warm wax used to remove hair from the skin. The wax is contained in a cartridge container with a disposable applicator which rolls the wax onto the skin's surface. A new applicator is used for each client.

Route of entry The three ways a chemical can enter the body are through ingestion (the mouth), inhalation (the nose), and absorption (the skin).

S

Sale and Supply of Goods Act (1994) This Act replaced the Sale of Goods Act (1982). Goods must be as described, of merchantable, satisfactory quality, and fit for their intended purpose.

Salon requirements Workplace procedures that ensure the smooth running of the business and compliance with any legislation, codes of practice etc.

Salon services Covers all the services offered in your workplace.

Sanitation The prevention of the multiplication of micro-organisms by cleansing or washing hands. This has a limited effect on the sanitation of an area as it does not kill all micro-organisms.

Saphenous vein A vein in the leg.

Sauna A service room of timber construction where the air inside is heated to produce a therapeutic effect on the body.

Saunarium A combination of the dry sauna and a wet steam room. The saunarium provides regulated heat and humidity with a temperature between 50–60°C and humidity between 40–50%. Further features include the addition of essential oils, essences and fibre optic lighting.

Scissors Nail tools used to shorten the length of the nail before filing.

Sculptured nails Artificial nails created by building the artificial nail onto the natural nail and extending it over a form rather than a plastic tip.

Sebaceous gland

Sebaceous gland A minute sac-like organ usually associated with the hair follicle which is referred to then as the pilo-sebaceous unit. The cells of the gland decompose and produce the skin's natural oil sebum. Sebaceous glands are found in the skin all over the body, except for the soles of the feet and the palms of the hands.

Sebum The skin's natural oil produced by the sebaceous glands. The cells of the glands decompose, producing sebum. Sebum moisturises and lubricates the skin keeping it supple, preventing it from drying out and plays a protective role. Sebum is composed of fatty acids and waxes. These have bactericidal and fungicidal properties, and so discourage the multiplication of micro-organisms on the surface of the skin.

Secondary infection Bacterial penetration into the skin causing infection.

Self-tan products Cosmetic products containing an ingredient which gives an artificial healthy, tanned appearance to the skin. Different methods can be used to apply self-tan products including spray, manual and airbrush application.

Semi-precious stones Crystals and semi-precious stones can be used within the stone therapy service. Each semi-precious stone is said to have unique characteristics, effects and uses. Often, a semi-precious stone is placed on the chakras during stone therapy. A stone is chosen to match the colour of the chakra, so that it can help 'open' the chakra.

Sensitivity The ability to react to a stimulus which can be used in reference to the body's immune system.

Sensitization The biological process of becoming sensitive to a chemical that usually results in an allergic reaction.

Sensory nerve endings These nerves receive information and relay this to the brain. They are found near the skin's surface and respond to touch, pressure, temperature and pain.

Service/treatment plan The stages or plan you intend to follow for carrying out a particular treatment to meet the agreed objectives, following the consultation and diagnostic procedures.

Shader A make-up product that minimizes and draws attention away from facial features.

Shaft (hair) The part of the hair that can be seen above the skin's surface extending from the hair follicle.

Sharps Sharp objects are referred to as 'sharps' and may have bye-laws covering their correct disposal as items of clinical waste. Sharps include scissors, needles used for electrical epilation and micro lances used for milia extraction or ingrown hair removal.

Shoulder girdle bones A type of connective tissue that provides attachment for the muscles which move the arms and includes the clavicle and scapula.

Shower experience A treatment which offers different shower sensations and is likened to a stimulating and invigorating cold fog mist or a warm tropical rainfall, that massages the skin.

Shower hydro An automated water massage with variable applications affecting temperature, application features and the pressure applied specifically to different body parts and reflex regions.

Side wall A soft tissue along the sides of the nail plate.

Single lashes Single artificial lashes which are attached to a single natural eyelash by use of adhesive.

Skeletal muscle The type of muscle connected to the skeleton.

Skeletal system Supports the softer tissues of the body and maintains the shape of the body.

Ski-jump nail A nail plate that curves upwards from the cuticle area to the free edge.

Skin allergy If the skin is sensitive to a particular substance an allergic skin reaction will occur. This is recognized by irritation, swelling and inflammation.

Skin analysis Assessment of the client's skin type and condition.

Skin appendages Structures within the skin including sweat glands (that excrete sweat), hair follicles (that produce hair), sebaceous glands (that produce the skin's natural oil, sebum) and nails (a horny substance that protects the ends of the fingers and toes).

Skin characteristics While looking at the skin type, additional characteristics may be seen. These include skin signs that indicate it may also be sensitive, dehydrated, moist or oedematous (puffy).

Skin removal Accidental removal of the upper, dead, protective cornified layer of the skin, leaving the granular layer exposed.

Skin sensitivity test A test performed to assess the skin's tolerance and sensitivity to a particular substance or service. This will confirm whether a client is suitable for a particular treatment before it is carried out and will prevent a contra-action occurring such as an allergic reaction.

Skin tags Fibrous hypertrophy skin growth projecting from the skin's surface and varying in size and colour. Skin tags are also referred to as pendunculated papilloma, fibro epithelial papilloma or polyp or raised fibroma simplex. These are commonly located on the neck axilla and groin area.

Skin tone The strength and elasticity of the skin.

Skin type The different physiological functioning of each person's skin indicates their skin type. Skin types include normal (balanced – neither dry or oily) dry (lacking in oil), oily (excessive oil) and combination (a mixture of two skin types, e.g. dry and oily).

Skin warming devices Techniques used to warm, cleanse and soften the skin to improve blood and lymphatic circulation. Skin warming makes the skin more receptive to further treatment and warming devices include facial electrical steamers and hot towel cabinets to heat hot towels.

Skull bones

Skull bones A type of connective tissue forming a hard structure. It surrounds and protects the brain and forms an attachment point for muscles. These include the occipital, frontal, parietal, temporal, sphenoid and ethmoid.

SMART An acronym used for setting objectives. **S**pecific, **M**easurable, **A**chievable, **R**ealistic **T**ime-bound.

Smile line A curve on the nail that is created naturally by the hyponychium or a coloured artificial overlay or nail polish.

Smooth muscle A type of muscle, associated with movement, that performs automatic functions of the body. These muscles are found in the digestive tract of the small intestine and move food by peristalsis action, etc.

Solehorn The epidermis attached to the underside of some natural nails. It is more often seen on nails that are almond shaped. It has a blood and nerve supply, so should not be removed.

Solvents Substances capable of dissolving other substances. Water is the 'universal solvent'.

Spa Derived from a village near Liege, in Belgium, called Spau, which had mineral hot springs that people would visit to improve their health and ailments. It refers today to a place where people can find a wide range of treatments used for their beneficial effects on the whole body. The spa environment and spa treatments induce a physical and mental sense of well-being.

Spa pool The client sits in a pool of warm water. Jets of air pass through the water under pressure through small openings in the bath creating bubbles which strike and massage the skin surface.

Spa services Used to induce a physical and mental sense of wellbeing.

Special occasion make-up Applied to suit the occasion for which it is to be seen and worn, such as a wedding.

Specialist skincare service products Additional skincare preparations available to target improvement. These products include eye gels, throat creams and ampoule services.

Spider Neavi (Telangiectasia Angioma) Dilated blood vessels, with smaller dilated capillaries radiating from them, like a spider's legs, from a central point.

Spleen An organ in the lymphatic system in the upper left side of the abdomen.

Splinter haemorrhage Small black streaks under the nail plate.

Spray-gun Equipment used to apply liquid self-tanning preparation to the skin.

Square A shape of the free edge of a nail that has a straight edge with corners and parallel sides.

Squoval A shape of the free edge of a nail that has corners and parallel sides but a rounded edge.

Steam room Water is heated and the steam created enters the steam room where the water vapour circulates. Steam is a wet heat treatment which cleanses the skin. The muscles of the body are also relaxed due to the rise in body temperature and increased blood circulation.

Steam service A warming effect created by boiling water, which is then vaporized and used on the skin to achieve both cleansing and stimulation.

Sterilization A process that achieves the complete destruction of all living organisms.

Stock-keeping Maintenance of stock levels to anticipate needs. Stock records note how much stock has been used and when a new order is needed. This may be achieved using manual or computerized systems.

Stop point The part of a plastic tip that fits around the free edge of the natural nail.

Stratum corneum The uppermost layer of the epidermis consisting of keratinized dead skin cells.

Stratum germinativum The base layer of the epidermis where new skin cells are formed.

Stratum granulosum One of the middle layers of the epidermis where the process of keratinization starts.

Stratum lucidum One of the middle layers of the epidermis apparent in the palms of the hands and soles of the feet.

Stratum spinosum One of the middle layers of the epidermis where some cells are connected together.

Strength The ability of a substance to withstand breakage if force is applied.

Stress A condition which develops when a person becomes pressurized. This may result in undesirable side-effects such as insomnia, muscular tension and skin disorders.

Stretch marks (striations) Scarring of the skin as a result of the skin breaking beneath the surface in the dermal layer.

Striated muscle A skeletal muscle that has stripes that cause movement of parts of the skeleton.

Strip sugar A system of wax depilation similar to the warm-wax technique, used to remove hair from the skin. Made from sugar, lemons and water, the sugar wax is applied to the skin, and is then removed using a wax removal strip.

Stye A bacterial infection of the sebaceous glands of the eyelash hair follicles. Small lumps appear on the inner rim of the eyelid and contain pus.

Stylist A professional who selects the clothing and accessories, dresses the model, and checks that the clothing ties in with the overall look to meet the design plan.

Subcutaneous layer A layer of adipose fatty tissue situated below the epidermis and dermis.

Sugar paste A system of wax depilation. An organic paste made from sugar, lemons and water is used to embed the hair when moved over the skin. The hair is removed from the skin when the paste is removed.

Sugaring A popular ancient method of hair removal using organic substances such as sugar and lemon. This system of depilation includes the use of sugar paste and/or strip sugar.

Sun damage

Sun damage Damage to the skin where the skin has created permanent melanin discoloration, e.g. freckles.

Superfluous hair Hair considered to be in excess of normal downy hair for the person's age and sex and is considered unwanted.

Supination An anatomical term describing a type of body movement where the body part moves upwards. For example, the supination of the hand turns the palm upwards by movement of the flexed forearm.

Sweat A liquid produced by the sweat glands in the skin. One of the main functions of sweat is to help regulate body temperature.

Sweat glands or sudoriferous glands Small tubes in the skin of the dermis and epidermis which excrete sweat. Their function is to regulate body temperature through the evaporation of sweat from the skin's surface. There are two types of sweat glands: the eccrine gland and the apocrine gland.

Synovial joints A type of movable joint.

System In this context, this refers to the 'system' used to overlay the natural nail or plastic tip, e.g. acrylic, UV gel, fibre.

Systemic disorder A disease caused by one of the systems of the body and affecting many areas.

Systemic medical condition A medical condition caused by a defect in one of the body's organs, e.g. the heart.

T

Talus A bone in the ankle.

Tapered A shape of the free edge where the nail becomes thinner towards the distal edge.

Tapotement Massage movements performed in a brisk, stimulating manner to increase blood supply and improve the tone of the skin and muscles. Movements include clapping and tapping. Also known as percussion.

Tapping A stone therapy technique which involves holding a stone on the body while rhythmically tapping with another to create a vibrational effect.

Target A goal to achieve usually within a timescale.

Tarsals Bones in the ankle.

Teamwork Supportive work by a group of people.

Telangiectasia Capillaries near the surface of the skin that are permanently dilated. Commonly known as thread veins.

Telogen The resting stage of the hair growth cycle where the hair is finally shed.

Tendons A type of connective tissue that connects muscles to bones.

Tepidarium (relaxation room) The relaxation room enables the client to rest between experiencing different spa treatments. This allows the body temperature and blood pressure to lower. The air is ambient, the same as the body's temperature, and is dry air to enhance the body's immune system and relieve stress. Heated couches may also be provided with soft lighting and relaxing music.

Terminal hair Deep-rooted, thick, coarse, pigmented hair found on the scalp, underarms, pubic region, eyelash and brow areas.

Test patch An assessment method used to determine the skin's tolerance to products or treatments. This may include a patch test, thermal test or tactile test.

Thalasso-pool A pool with warm water hydro jets (approximately 33°C in temperature) with a 3% salt content to simulate sea water.

Thalassotherapy The therapeutic use of marine products including sand, algae, marine silt, air and sea water rich in minerals to restore the balance and health of the body. Thalassotherapy centres are built within a 500 metre radius of the seaside. When thalassotherapy is sited inland, it is referred to as thalasso.

Thermal booties Electrically heated boots where the feet are placed following the application of a skin service product such as a mask. The heat aids the absorption of the product and improves skin functioning.

Thermal mitts Electrically heated gloves where the hands are placed following the application of a skin service product such as a mask. The heat aids the absorption of the product and improves skin functioning.

Thermal sensitivity test A test to assess the skin's tolerance to heat and to confirm that it can differentiate between different temperatures. It is used as a safety check before certain services are carried out. This test is performed before wax application to check that the temperature of the wax is not too warm. The wax is tested by the therapist on themselves, usually on the inner wrist, and then on the client.

Thermometer Equipment used to measure temperature.

Thixotropic The ability of a liquid to become thinner in viscosity when agitated and return to its original viscosity when the agitation stops.

Tibia A bone of the lower leg.

Tinea corporis or body ringworm A fungal infection of the skin where small, scaly red patches spread outwards and then heal from the centre, leaving a ring.

Tinea pedis or athlete's foot A fungal infection of the foot that occurs in the webs of the skin between the toes. Small blisters form which later burst. The skin in the area can become dry with a scaly appearance.

Tinea unguium A fungal infection of the nails. The nail turns yellowish-grey in colour.

Tissues Groups of cells, sharing function, shape and size that specialize in carrying out particular functions. These include: epithelial, connective, muscular and nervous tissue.

Toluenediamine Small molecules of permanent dye used in a tinting service.

Toning lotion A skincare preparation formulated to treat the different skin types and facial characteristics. It is applied to remove all traces of cleanser from the skin. It produces a cooling effect and has a tightening effect on the skin.

Tonsils A prominent mass of lymphatic tissue located at the back of the throat.

Top coat A nail polish product applied over another nail polish to provide additional strength and durability to the finish.

Top note A measure of the highest evaporation rate of an essential oil. These commonly have a sharp aroma and a stimulating effect.

Topical anaesthetic Cream applied to an area of skin to reduce pain and symptoms of discomfort. Manufacturer's instructions must always be followed.

Towel steaming An alternative to facial steaming which uses an electrical vapour unit. Small, clean facial towels are heated in a bowl of warm water or specialized heater before application to the face to warm, cleanse and stimulate the skin.

Toxic The description of a substance that can adversely harm humans at measured levels.

Trade Descriptions Acts (1968 and 1972) Legislation that states that information provided when selling products, both in written and verbal form, should be accurate.

Transverse furrows A nail condition where grooves appear on the nail, running from side to side.

Trauma The result of excessive force.

Travellers' cheques An alternative form of payment used when travelling abroad and must be compared with the client's passport.

Treatment plan The stages or plan you intend to follow when carrying out a particular treatment to meet the agreed objectives following a consultation and diagnostic procedures.

Trigger point (stone therapy technique) Deep, continuous pressure with a stone on an isolated area to achieve relief of muscular tension.

Tucking (stone therapy technique) A warm stone is positioned underneath an area of the body after it has been used for service (e.g. knees, legs, shoulder, etc.).

Turnover The monetary value of total sales over a set period.

Tweezers Small metal tools used to remove body hair by pulling the hair from the bottom of the hair follicle (the small opening in the skin where the hair grows from). There are two types of tweezers: automatic – designed to remove the bulk of the hair, and manual – designed to remove the stray hairs.

Two-piece needle A needle made from two pieces of joined metal. The needle has three parts: the shank, shaft and tip. A two-piece needle is less sturdy that a one-piece needle.

U

Ulna A bone of the lower arm.

Ulnar artery and vein An artery and vein in the lower arm.

Ultraviolet light (UVL) Invisible rays in the light spectrum with a wavelength shorter than visible light rays. UV waves can be divided into three types according to their wavelengths: UVA, UVB and UVC.

Upper arch The curve of the nail from the cuticle area to the free edge.

Urinary system The excretory system which filters waste products from the blood to maintain its normal composition. Waste material is filtered out of the blood by the kidneys and made into urine.

UV absorbers Additives that act like sunscreens.

UV block A chemical ingredient that prevents UV rays from affecting the product or underlying skin tissues.

UV gel One of the 'systems' of artificial nails. It uses a pre-mixed 'gel' and UV light to create the overlay.

UV light cured The process of polymerization using a photoinitator (usually UV light) to start the chemical reaction.

UV tanning The skin is exposed to artificially produced UV light and the skin darkens creating a tan. Artificial UV is produced by high or low-pressure tubes and lamps. The term pressure relates to the wattage (power or energy) of the lamps.

V

Vacuum suction service A mechanical service which can be applied to the face or body. External suction is applied to the surface tissues causing lift and stimulation of the underlying tissues. Locally, blood and lymphatic circulation is improved which aids the removal of any tissue fluid that has accumulated. Vacuum suction service also improves skin texture and appearance.

Vapour unit An electrical appliance that heats water to produce steam which is applied to the face and neck to warm, cleanse and stimulate the skin.

Vapours Gas molecules of a chemical in the air created by the evaporation of the substance.

Varicose veins Veins whose valves have become weak and lost their elasticity. The area appears knotted, swollen and bluish/purple in colour. Varicose veins are usually seen in the legs.

Vein Blood vessels that contain valves and return the blood towards the heart.

Vellus hair Hair which is fine, downy and soft and found on the face and body. Vellus hair does not always have a medulla.

Vena cava A large vein leading to the heart.

Ventilation The process of cleaning the air in an area and therefore removing dust, carbon dioxide and vapours.

Ventricle (right and left) The two lower chambers of the heart that pump the blood to the lungs and arteries of the body.

Verbal communication Occurs when you talk to another person, either face to face or over the telephone.

Verruca or plantar wart A viral infection where small epidermal skin growths appear, either raised or flat depending upon their location, and have a rough surface. Verrucas are similar to warts, but are ingrowing and usually found on the feet.

Vibrations massage Manipulation used to relieve pain and fatigue. It is applied to a nerve centre to stimulate the nerves and produce a sedative effect. The movements are firm and trembling, performed with one or both hands.

Virilization A condition where the female body becomes more masculine resulting in heavy facial and body hair growth in a masculine pattern.

Viruses Minute entities, too small to see even under an ordinary microscope. They are considered to be parasites, as they require living tissue in order to survive. Viruses invade healthy body cells and multiply within the cell. In due course the cell walls break down, liberating new viral particles to attack further cells, and therefore the infection spreads.

Viscosity The measure of a liquid's ability to flow. Its thinness or thickness.

Vitamin D A fatty substance in the skin converted to vitamin D with UV light from the sun. It is essential for the efficient absorption and use of calcium. Vitamin D circulates in the blood and, with the mineral salts calcium and phosphorus, helps the formation and maintenance of the body's bones.

Vitiligo A condition of the skin where it is not able to produce the pigment melanin resulting in pigment absence.

Volatile A description of a substance that easily evaporates in air.

Voluntary nervous system The part of the nervous system that is under conscious control.

VRQ Vocationally Related Qualification. A competence based qualification achieved through a process of assessment and examination. It is based on the National Occupational Standards and is strongly promoted by the Department for Education and Employment.

W

Warm wax A system of wax depilation. Warm wax remains soft at body temperature. It is frequently made of mixtures of glucose syrup and zinc oxide. Honey can be used instead of glucose syrup; this is referred to as honey wax. It is removed from the skin with a wax removal strip.

Warm-oil service Involves gently heating a small amount of oil and soaking the nails and cuticles in it to nourish the nails and soften the cuticles and surrounding skin.

Warts Small epidermal infectious skin growths which may be raised or flat and are caused by a viral infection.

Waste Items, substances and materials requiring disposal following a service. Waste must be disposed of safely to meet the legal and salon requirements. Clinical waste is waste derived from human tissues. This includes blood and tissue fluids and should be disposed of as recommended by the Environment Agency in accordance with the Controlled Waste (Amendment) Regulations (1993).

Watery eyes Over-secretion of tears from the eyes which would normally drain into the nasal cavity.

Wax depilation The temporary removal of excess hair from a body part using wax.

Waxing The use of wax to remove hairs temporarily from the face and body.

Waxing products Cosmetic preparations used for a waxing service which have specific benefits to cleanse the skin, assist in hair removal care and improve the appearance and healing properties of the skin following hair removal.

Wet area A spa area where all water based equipment and treatments are provided including the sauna, steam room, spa pool etc.

Wet flotation A spa treatment where the body is suspended in water. The treatment uses Epsom salts diluted in water at a high concentration, which enables the body to float and be suspended in the water, inducing physical and mental relaxation.

White-tip powder A white acrylic powder used to create a white free edge on an artificial nail.

Whitlow Localized and painful swelling at the edge of the nail plate.

Work techniques The methods used to carry out services.

Workplace The environment where you perform your duties of work e.g. your salon.

Workplace (Health Safety and Welfare) Regulations (1992) These regulations provide the employer with an approved code of practice for maintaining a safe, secure working environment that meets the needs of all employees.

Workplace policies Documentation prepared by your employer on the procedures to be followed in your workplace. Examples are your employer's safety policy statement, or general health and safety statements and written safety procedures covering aspects of the workplace that should be drawn to the employees' (and 'other persons'') attention, pricing policies and customer service policies.

Workplace practices Any activities, procedures, use of materials or equipment and working techniques used to carry out your job. Lifting techniques and maintaining good posture while working are also included.

Wrap fabrics Nail enhancement material used to overlay the natural nail to provide strength e.g fibreglass, silk etc.

Y

Yeast A type of fungus. Some yeasts can cause fungal infections.

Z

Zones The three areas of the artificial nail referred to when creating the correct artificial structure.